Rose Petals
and
Muddy Footprints

Rose Petals
and
Muddy Footprints

An Autobiography

PETER BEALES

2008

© Peter Beales Roses Ltd 2008

The right of Peter Beales to be identified
as the author of this work has been asserted by him
in accordance with the Copyright, Designs
and Patents Act, 1988

First published in Great Britain 2008
by Peter Beales Roses Ltd

Page makeup in Sabon by Waveney Typesetters
Wymondham, Norfolk
Printed and bound in Great Britain
by Biddles Ltd, King's Lynn, Norfolk

TO THE MEMORY OF
EVELYN MAY

Contents

Author's Note

Writing the story of my life is something I have always wanted to do but – for reasons that will become apparent as the text unfolds – it would not have been possible while my mother was alive. Mum passed away, at the age of ninety, in the summer of 2006 and even now I hesitate to make this story public; but deep down inside me I know she would have approved. It has not been easy to bare my soul: nevertheless what you are about to read is my life – warts and all.

I am most grateful to all those who have made my task a little easier. In particular my wife Joan, for not only putting the text onto the computer but for her valuable help as an aide-mémoire and for being such a support at all times. In addition I must thank Mandy, Richard and Debbie for their encouragement and proof-reading. Thanks too to my staff for holding the fort during my absences, to Pete Henshall for his expertise with the computer, and to Julia Richardson and Jackie Duffy for their design skills. I am indebted also to Michael Russell for his advice on the presentation of the text and for guiding me through the business aspects relating to publication.

I

The Early Years

Through hazy memories of early childhood I vaguely recollect an elderly lady hanging laundry on the washing line to dry. She was my maternal grandmother. Near to the pram or pushchair in which I sat I can remember seeing a rose, a pink rose. This lovely lady passed away while I was still a child, so I never did have the chance to ask her if she knew the name of that rose. However, from time to time over the years, I have cast my mind back and have now concluded that it was probably 'Dorothy Perkins' for then, as now, it was one of the most commonly grown ramblers. It propagates easily from cuttings, and I would imagine this is how she acquired it, perhaps from a friend. Even then roses were expensive and I very much doubt if she would have been able to afford to buy one.

Nanny Beales, 'Nan' I called her, with her husband George, 'Granddad', brought me up, from the day I was born until I was eight, as part of their family. Living with us then were their teenage children Ethel, John and Walter. Several years earlier their firstborn George had died from scarlet fever at the age of eight. Also part of the family was Nan's niece Sheila who came to live with them after her mother died in the early 1930s. Sheila was ten when I came along. Their middle daughter Dorothy was working locally as a housekeeper. Their eldest daughter, Evelyn, my mother, had been in service to a family in London but returned home pregnant. Nan and the rest of the family, although upset at the 'disgrace', supported her and when I was born I became an inconvenient but nevertheless welcome addition to the family.

Nan was a homely lady of medium height and somewhat overweight in a cuddly sort of way. She had a chubby, smiling face. Although my memories of her are far from complete I recall that she had very long hair, down to her waist. During the day she would either wear it up in a bun or braided, with the plaits wound around her head in a sort of coronet, held in place by grips. Its colour was on the whiter side of grey. Although I now realise that I took advantage of her placid nature far too much, our relationship was always very loving and I felt secure in her company.

Soon after my birth my mother had to go to work to support me and so she found a position as a live-in housemaid in the home of a wealthy farmer in the village. This meant that Auntie Ethel, then aged thirteen or fourteen, had to take me to Mum for my feeds and therefore Mum could only see me for any length of time on her one 'day-off' each week. Meanwhile the family must have had to put up with lots of gossip and tittle-tattle from the locals. In those days it was considered shameful to have a child out of wedlock and I can now well imagine the whispering and speculation that must have gone on. My illegitimacy was kept secret within the family for years and I did not find out about it myself until I was well into my teens.

My grandparents had to live through some difficult times in their life and my arrival must have seemed to them like one more burden in their struggle to make ends meet. In 1936, when I was born, they were tenants of a smallholding called May Farm in the little village of Banningham, situated in a delightful part of North Norfolk between the market towns of North Walsham and Aylsham. To take on this tenancy they had invested money awarded to Granddad as compensation following a freak accident that had happened five years earlier.

One day, while bringing in the corn harvest, Granddad was accidentally stabbed in the face with a pitchfork, causing loss of sight to one eye. He was standing on a wagon, loading the sheaves whilst the farmer tossed them up to him for stacking. Granddad turned to receive a forkful of sheaves and, somehow, the prongs of the pitchfork caught his eye. After a day or two in a local hospital he was moved to a specialist eye hospital in London. They could not, however, save his eye. After several weeks he returned home. Granddad had been a farm worker ever since leaving the Army in 1919 and it was the only job he knew. The farmer said that he would find him work on the farm but Granddad felt uncomfortable about this because to accept meant that he would be under an obligation to the farmer; I suppose he was just too proud for his own good.

A farm-worker's eye was obviously not worth much in those days, for the powers that be, whoever they were, awarded Granddad the grand sum of two hundred and fifty pounds compensation. Furthermore their generosity even extended to the payment of ten shillings a week as a disability pension. Two hundred and fifty pounds probably seemed like a small fortune to someone previously earning only a few shillings a week. Without seeking any financial advice he obviously thought it would be enough to take on the tenancy of a smallholding. Becoming his own boss was something that few manual workers then could ever hope to achieve.

From the moment I was born I was the 'apple' of Granddad's one eye, so much so that he used to call me 'Pippin', a name which caught on and which I lived with right up to the time I left school. I understand that there were two reasons for this nickname, first, because my cheeks were as rosy as an apple and secondly because we had a dog called Peter and when one of us was called the other would come too. Even now, when I meet up with long lost cousins or old school chums, I'm amused when they greet me by this name. My mother continued to call me 'Pippin' until the day she died.

Two years after I was born Mum met a farm worker who was employed on the farm where she was housekeeper. His name was Walter Howes; he was twenty-six years older than her and still lived with his parents, his mother being an invalid confined to a wheelchair. A little while later they were married and after the wedding Mum took me back to live with them all, Walter having said 'I marry the girl, I marry the boy'. Obviously I cannot recall what happened then but it would seem that a month or so later Granddad Beales came to visit us. To this day I don't know what he discovered to make him act in the in the way he did but apparently he put me on the crossbar of his bicycle and took me back to live with him and Nan at May Farm.

I do not remember much about Granddad. If I try really hard I can see someone with a large moustache, wearing a cloth cap and riding an old bicycle with a carrier on the front. I can also recall sitting on the crossbar of that bike en route with him to wherever. In those days bicycles were a common mode of transport used by the working class for taking children around with them. Some bikes even had special little seats fixed to their crossbars for this purpose. I remember, too, riding in a pony and trap beside a man who seemed old to me: Granddad?

I have since been told by my Aunt Ethel that Nan and Granddad tried very hard to make their little farm work but it was just too small and the soil too impoverished to support a large family. A story still told within the family is that Nan had a long-standing friend who regularly drove a train between North Walsham and Aylsham. The railway line ran alongside one of the fields at May Farm and as it chugged past her friend would throw out a couple of large lumps of coal, alerting her with a blast or two on the whistle. Illegal or not, this helped to keep the home warm at this time of coal rationing.

My aunt went on to tell me that when it became clear that the little farm only brought in a meagre income, in order to make ends meet, Granddad used the family's pony and trap to hawk wet fish and shellfish around the nearby villages. The fish, purchased from a wholesale fishmonger at Great Yarmouth, was sent to North Walsham by train two or three times a week, from where it was collected by Granddad. My grandparents struggled on as long as they could but, in the end, were forced to cut their losses and move. By then their son John had returned home from working on the trawlers in the North Sea. In those days Great Yarmouth and Lowestoft were the home ports for large fleets of trawlers and drifters fishing for herrings and mackerel. Because of Granddad's disability and deteriorating health Uncle John became the main family breadwinner and found a job as a farm worker at Binny's Farm, Felmingham. With it came a tied house called Heath Farmhouse in Cucumber Lane.

The new house seemed huge to me, much bigger than May Farm, with lots more rooms. Barns and sheds outside beckoned me to explore and play in them. It was a perfect place for an active boy to live. One thing that stands out in my memory is that the house had what I then thought of as a tin roof and, when it rained heavily, the noise of the rain hitting the roof sounded like a machine-gun. I would lie in bed pretending the Germans had come, for there was much talk of war in the household at that time. I now know that the corrugated iron was covering an old thatched roof.

There was an ancient pear tree growing outside the house with its branches close to one of the bedroom windows and I recall once clambering out of this window onto the tree and trying to climb down to the ground. My cousin Sheila also used this means of escape when she wanted to sneak off to dances in the village or to visit her friends. Sheila was taller than I was and I could not reach the stronger branches that she used. The branches I could reach were far too flimsy to bear my weight and I ended up flat on my face on the grass below with lots of scratches and a big dent in my pride.

I was only four when Granddad became ill with severe tummy pains and was taken to the Norfolk and Norwich Hospital. I was told later that he died while on the operating table. Apparently he had had a strangulated hernia. He was then only sixty years old. On the day he passed away war was declared and Uncle John, who had been in the Territorial Army for some time, was called up. Such was the discipline in the Army at that time that he was only allowed a few hours' leave to attend his father's funeral a few days later. He was also given permission to wear a black armband over his uniform. With war only just having been declared, his superiors would not grant him compassionate leave, in spite of the fact that he was billeted in the town of North Walsham, where the funeral took place. When I learned about this many years later I was totally horrified by the apparent intransigence and inhumanity of the then severe military discipline.

Try as I may I cannot actually remember Granddad's funeral but I can recall a period of much sadness and crying in the household and also of being taken to a grave, presumably his, by my aunts. I am told that a great-aunt looked after me while the funeral took place and when I asked her where Granddad had gone, she replied 'To see God.' 'Oh, I know who you mean,' I said, 'Mr Goddard is the man Nan gets her meat from.'

Soon after Granddad's demise Uncle John was posted to the fated Fifth Battalion of the Royal Norfolk Regiment; fated, because when the troop carrier with the entire battalion on board sailed into Singapore harbour, it was immediately captured by the Japanese who had taken the island only hours before. This meant that Uncle John, with the rest of his battalion, spent the entire war building the

Burma Railway for their captors. Under the harsh conditions endured by prisoners of war there he, like many others, was struck down with dysentery and died. Thus, before I had a chance to get to know him he disappeared from my life. His younger brother Walter was just ten years old when I was born and so became much more like a big brother to me than an uncle. I recall many happy hours in his company, being taught to play cricket and to kick a ball; not to mention playing conkers and riding for miles on the crossbar of his bike. Uncle Walter and I remained good friends throughout the years until he passed away in the 1980s, far too early, at the age of sixty-four.

2

And So to School

I knew that when I was five I would have to go to school and, all too soon, the dreaded day dawned, the day I became a pupil at the little primary school in the nearby village of Colby. Like, I imagine, any other child just starting school, I was very nervous. That morning the face washing, tooth-cleaning ritual seemed to be exaggerated and my hair, nails and clothes were subjected to a rigid inspection. Nan had packed me up a lunch which she placed in an old, well-worn satchel passed down to me from Uncle Walter who had left school at the age of fourteen. It was Aunt Ethel who took me to school and although on the way I tried to put on a brave face, when we arrived at the school I'm afraid I threw a tantrum and refused to go in. Soon one of the teachers came and took me by the hand and marched me into the classroom.

Trying to make up for my mother's absence, my grandparents and aunts had thoroughly spoiled me and I remember having a very hard time at school – I was being disciplined for the first time in my life. I had always been used to getting my own way and resented being told what to do. My teachers appeared to me to be very strict. I remember they would walk between the desks whilst teaching us and woe betide any child caught fidgeting or whispering. To my knowledge though none of them ever lifted a finger against any of us but we all believed they were more than capable of doing so should the need arise.

I played truant as often as I could, spending days just meandering through meadows, hiding in hedgerows and cornfields or fishing for sticklebacks with a jam jar on a piece of string in the shallow stream close to the school. I can also remember sitting beneath the bridge over the stream at Banningham with my feet dangling in the water aimlessly whiling away the time. As a rule I got away with these spells of truancy. In 2006, as an old boy of

Colby School I was asked if I would name a rose to celebrate the school's centenary. I was honoured to do so and when I returned there to present the rose I found myself thinking that the discipline I had experienced there had probably been the making of me.

The walk to and from school was three miles each way, so not actually turning up was an easy option. Even when Aunt Ethel took me, I would go into the playground and hide in the toilets for a while until the bell went and then I would run off, to anywhere but school. Time did not seem to matter. I came to enjoy my own company and spent ages and ages daydreaming of an idyllic world far beyond the confines of my simple rural existence. In this world I re-enacted some of the stories I had had read to me by Nan and my aunts. Stories of highwaymen and giants as well characters I had seen in comics such as *Film Fun*. In this fantasy world I was always the hero, I was the one that everyone looked up to and, furthermore, I always got my own way.

The reality of time only came into being when I noticed the other children making their way home. I would follow some distance behind them to give the illusion that I had also been at school all day. Fortunately Heath Farm was relatively isolated and I used to take a short cut across the fields, arriving home at the expected time. Sometimes, if it had been raining, I would take off my shoes and socks to walk through the meadows to give the impression that I had been walking along the road.

If I felt hungry while I was playing truant, I would appease my appetite by gathering what I could find in the hedgerows and fields. In the spring I nibbled the tips of the young shoots of hawthorn trees. Known as 'bread and cheese', these have a nutty flavour and are quite pleasing to the taste buds. I also broke off the young tips of the dog rose and peeled back the bark to expose the soft, sweet-tasting pith beneath. Later on in the summer I found wild strawberries and chewed on the succulent, bittersweet leaves of the wood sorrel.

Autumn was a good time for playing truant as I knew where to find hazelnuts and chestnuts as well as blackberries. When I was feeling a little more adventurous I occasionally scrumped apples from gardens in the village and I knew of a walnut tree that, although it meant breaking cover, was far too tempting to ignore. This wayward behaviour went on for at least three years and I now realise what a difficult child I must have been. Thank goodness I had not been born in a city for I am sure I would have ended up a delinquent. Now I am older I often wonder why my frequent spells away from school were never reported to my family. I can only assume that the school inspectors were thin on the ground during wartime.

During my years at Colby School I, like all the people of Norfolk, lived almost constantly with the noise of hundreds of planes assembling in the skies over the county in readiness to fly across the North Sea to bomb Germany. On fine days the outline of each plane was clearly visible as they circled to form themselves into a mass armada in preparation for their departure. Such was their density that I was always amazed that they didn't collide. In the daytime the planes were American from the various American air bases scattered over East Anglia; a few hours later towards the end of the day those that had not met with misfortune returned home in a less orderly manner. It all started again as it got dark but, at night, it was the turn of the Royal Air Force.

Living at Heath Farm had developed my sense of adventure and I used to spend hours, whenever I could, exploring the countryside within walking distance of home. From the age of seven new territories opened up for me as I learned to ride a bicycle. Some of my happiest hours were spent exploring Felmingham Heath, an area of about fifty acres, which seemed vast to me then.

The Heath consists largely of gorse and scrub with a few trees. It is full of wild life from rabbits to squirrels and numerous species of birds; in particular I recall the yellowhammers – at least I now know this is what they were. Sweethearts used the Heath for courting and, from time to time, the Army carried out manoeuvres there. I resented both these very different intrusions into what I thought of as my territory. Courting couples threatened all sorts of punishments if I didn't scarper and the Army barred my entry for the duration of their exercises, which could sometimes last for a whole week. I collected lots of spent cartridges and the occasional live .303 round; all of which I squirrelled away in a corner of our barn.

Speaking of the barn, I used to love to watch the bats swooping around the house at dusk, for they lived in the rafters of the barn and outbuildings. Believing that they were attracted by the scent of human hair, I used to toss my school cap into the air in the hope that I would catch one. I can't remember who told me the human hair fallacy but it never worked. At the entrance to Heath Farm, by the edge of the drive, there was a pond known as 'the pit'. Farm horses used to drink from this pond on their way to and from their work in the fields. In the spring it became the home of frogs, toads and newts. The pond was not deep. 'Keep away from that pit!' Nan used to shout, 'I don't want you to get too wet, or drown.'

Our nearest neighbour in Cucumber Lane was a Mr Cole who lived in a cottage just up the lane from us. He collected antiques and lots of interesting old bric-a-brac. From time to time I was allowed to look into the sheds in which all his precious paraphernalia was stored. I spent hours with my head stuck into bound copies of the *Illustrated London News*, dated from around the time of the South African Boer War. I had never seen a picture of a coloured person until then and the headdresses and necklaces worn by the Zulu warriors fascinated me, as did their spears. Many of the illustrations stimulated my imagination to the point of obsession, alternating between my triumph at having overcome the enemy or lying wounded and dying, a glorious hero. I think Mr Cole must have died because, suddenly, my visits to him and adventures amongst his books and objets d'art came to an abrupt end. For a long time I could not pass his house without thinking about all the treasures he had allowed me to share with him.

Having become used to my own company at the age of six, I didn't always totally behave myself even at home. On one occasion I recall taking the straw from the nest boxes in the chicken house and setting fire to it in the doorway. To do this I used an old magnifying glass that I held above the straw to capture the direct rays from the sun. The straw smouldered for a while and then burst into flame. Fortunately I had the presence of mind to chase out all the chickens before the fire got out of control and burned the wooden building to the ground. What a fire that was! I was exhilarated but at the same time terrified because I knew I would be in for it. From his demeanour I could tell that Uncle Walter thought it was quite funny, not so Nan. By the time I emerged from hiding her anger had abated somewhat and I got off with no more than a tongue lashing and being sent to bed with no supper.

Misadventures were numerous during those early childhood years. One morning, unknown to the driver, I had tried to steal a lift on the back of the lorry delivering milk to the school, by climbing on to the tailboard while it was moving off from a delivery. I ended up spreadeagled on the metalled road. I still have the scars on my knees and elbows to show for it. Then, while fruit picking one day, I was violently sick from eating too many blackcurrants and raspberries. I used to have to accompany Nan to the fruit fields each season in order for her to earn an extra shilling or two. I can still recall the distinctive pungent aroma of blackcurrant bushes. During fruit-picking season the whole family took part and there were lots of children of my age in the fields. We should have helped to pick the fruit but instead we played games such as cowboys and Indians amongst the currant bushes.

I must have been about five when the routine of our household was disrupted by a family of evacuees from the East End of London, their arrival causing a major upheaval. With their cockney accents and slick city personas they were quite different from our family, steeped as we were in the ways of the country. Each family found the other a novelty but, within a few weeks, these feelings had worn off and it became clear that tensions were building up between us all the time. The mother, Kath, bossed her two boys and me incessantly. They were older and craftier than I was and I came to resent their presence in our house and the aggravation they caused.

Our family tried very hard to accommodate these enforced lodgers because we, or at least the adults, understood that they had been evacuated from London to escape the Blitz. It became increasingly difficult however for Nan because by now she was far from well and Ethel and Walter were both working during the day. Nan was clearly unable to cope with the tensions and the demanding natures of our lodgers.

This was a difficult situation, for the husband and father of the evacuees was serving abroad in the forces. Being away from the eyes of her neighbours in London, his wife took advantage of her new-found freedom to entertain several boyfriends, Americans from a local air base, in our house. Nan tried to put a stop to this, without success. This woman even gave birth to a child while living with us, making life even more intolerable. Nan's health deteriorated quickly. I didn't know at the time that she had cancer of the bowel, and even if I had, I would not have known what it was. I knew that she was very ill when she was admitted to the Norfolk and Norwich Hospital, where she eventually died in 1945. I was just nine and I missed her dreadfully for she had always been there for me and her passing left a big gap in my life.

I can't remember much about Nan's funeral. I do remember riding in a car, in all probability the first time I had ever done so, presumably to the service. I know she is buried in the cemetery at North Walsham and I can just about recall being taken there to put flowers on her grave. At the time she died the war was coming to an end. I am told that the evacuees moved out after Nan passed away, much to the relief of the family. The welfare department of the local council found them a council house to live in because by now there were three children and their mother did not want to move back to London.

The next event of any significance in the Beales household was the marriage of my Aunt Ethel, then in her early twenties, to Ted, an Army sergeant in the Suffolk Regiment. The first time I met him I was impressed because he was wearing uniform. He was tall and good-looking. He became a regular visitor to Heath Farm and, together with Uncle Walter, taught me how to ride a bike. Their wedding took place in North Walsham church and all I can remember about the wedding ceremony is that I was dressed up to the nines as a pageboy. I can recall the reception though, the music and dancing and the ignominy of having to be taken home before the end. I was most upset and made quite a scene before being forcibly taken from the party by a member of the family.

3

A Rude Awakening

Things changed for me after Nan passed away. Aunt Ethel and her new husband took up residence at Heath Farm and wanted me to stay with them but my mother took me back to live with her. She and her family rented a smallholding called Meadow Farm in Buck Brigg, a little hamlet consisting of just four houses near to the village of Colby. I was just coming up to my ninth birthday.

My mother had been married to Walter Howes for two years when she gave birth to a daughter, whom he adored in spite of the fact that he had wanted a son. Walter chose the names Rosemary Ronald for her. Ronald because he was disappointed that she was a girl but also after one of his brothers who had been killed in a tragic accident with a circular saw a few years earlier. When I look back, I am convinced that my mother only married Walter Howes to give me a father. When I went to live there, the household consisted of Walter, Mum, Rosie, as she came to be called, and Walter's father (another Walter), who was then in his mid-seventies.

To a young boy of nine who had always been cosseted to the point of being spoiled, the move to Buck Brigg was a rude awakening. I missed Nan dreadfully, not really understanding why she had had to die and leave me. I was suddenly faced with a new and, to me, terrible change in my life. Half-sister Rosie, who was about seven years old when I moved in, did not help matters. We tormented each other whenever possible but I always seemed to be the one that was blamed – not surprising I suppose, as Rosie was Walter's own flesh and blood. Getting into trouble with him was not a pleasant experience.

I soon found out that he was a strict disciplinarian and I had to conform to a new set of rules: to be seen and not heard was one of the hardest adjustments I had to make. He was also a stickler for good timekeeping and I often received double punishment for turning up late for the evening meal. My ears would be boxed and I would be made to sit at the table without any food or drink until everybody else had finished and then sent to bed hungry. Mum would sometimes manage to sneak a sandwich or a couple of cakes into my bedroom for me. Had Walter known about this she would have received a severe tongue-lashing.

Although it was the late 1940s, Walter's Sunday best was what I now recognise as being fashionable dress in the 1920s. He wore a long Norfolk jacket and jodhpur-like trousers called breeches with a flap in the front, having a button on each of the top corners. With this he would wear a tight-fitting waistcoat and highly polished brown or black laced up boots. His shirts were collar-less and I never saw him without his bright red polka dot neckerchief. Even though he was in his mid forties at that time he did not have a grey hair on his head. He always wore a cloth cap at a rakish angle, both outdoors and in, even at mealtimes. On the very odd occasion when he did remove his cap, it was laid on the table beside him. His more casual clothes for weekdays were navy blue overalls with bib and braces. Over these he always wore the dreaded belt with a large brass buckle, 'strap' as he called it. As he got older presumably because his feet were sore, he mostly wore soft plimsolls or slippers.

Like many of his contemporaries he had a broad Norfolk accent and those who spoke 'proper' made fun of this. Many of my friends, and I myself, also 'spouk narfuc' but his accent sounded broader and we thought it comical. Our teachers tried to make us pronounce our words correctly. I now realise of course that many regional accents, including that of Norfolk, are in danger of being lost forever. Once a Norfolk man always a Norfolk man and now, from time to time, I deliberately colour my speech with the old Norfolk expressions such as 'howaryuh gittin on bor?'

My mother always had to make her own clothes and I can never recollect seeing her wearing anything new, except perhaps shoes, which always had to be sensible. Walter did not like her to wear make up or anything fancy. She wore a pinafore in the house. Whenever we could Mum and I found time to be alone together, away from my stepfather's dominance. On these occasions she was able to relax and display her naturally loving nature to me. What should have been a natural bond between mother and son was not allowed to blossom. She was not allowed to show any affection to me within the family unit because of Walter's possessiveness. I often teased Mum about her height, or lack of it. In her stockinged feet she was only four feet ten inches tall; from time to time I used to call her 'lofty'. When she was not under pressure she always wore a broad smile. Like mine, her hair was dark. She was an attractive little lady. Mum wore false teeth because she had lost all hers at the age of twenty when she was carrying me.

From his youth Walter had always ridden motorbikes and two or three of his old bikes were stored in one of the sheds at Meadow Farm. They were all belt-driven, water-cooled Levises of between 250 and 350cc. After these he moved on to an old prewar BSA and, apparently, one day while Mum was riding pillion behind Walter she sneezed violently and her false teeth shot out on to the road. Before Walter could turn the motorbike around and go back to retrieve them, they had been run over by a lorry and crushed to pieces.

Moving to Meadow Farm meant that I had to change schools so I started at Aldborough Primary School at the beginning of the autumn term 1945. I travelled to and from school in an old coach named the 'Red Rover'. It was a prewar Albion and rather prone to breaking down, much to the delight of its young passengers.

Something else that sticks in my memory is riding in a pony and trap to such events as village fetes and to carnivals and I clearly remember being taken to the polling station by this mode of transport for the adults to vote in the 1945 election. This resulted in much celebration in our household, for the Labour Party under Clement Atlee won a landslide victory. Naturally I had no understanding of politics so it seemed to me unfair that Winston Churchill was thrown out of office, for I knew that he had been our leader during the war. When I mentioned this to my mother she said 'Don't tell your father or grandfather because they support the Labour Party and believe that Churchill is nothing but a warmonger.'

I well remember that first day at Aldborough School. I was asked to read from an elementary book as a test of my abilities. I failed hopelessly for I could hardly write my name, let alone read: so, at the age of nine, I was put into the second year Infants where, at first,

I struggled. Looking back though, this is the best thing that could have happened to me, for it started me off at the level my brain had so far reached. Despite the derision of the older children I quickly grasped the basics and after the first three terms I was allowed to rejoin my own age group.

It was then that I came under the wing of a teacher called Mrs Hall. She seemed to understand instinctively that I was now ready to learn and move on. I spent a full year in the middle class under her guidance and I now believe that that year proved to be the turning point in my life. Somehow this gifted teacher was able to instil in me self-confidence, a belief in myself and a desire to do better. Even then I still had some way to go and the hierarchy of the school decided that I was not a candidate to sit the eleven plus examination. They were probably right but I must say I felt very resentful at the time, especially when some of my mates passed the examination and went on to grammar school.

The headmaster during my first years at Aldborough was a Mr Carter (we called him Billy). He was strict but fair and well respected by both pupils and parents. His school enjoyed a good reputation in the county for both educational and sporting achievement. I enjoyed taking part in sport but my performance was never more than average. I usually managed to scrape into the school teams at both football and cricket.

During my second year Billy Carter retired and, yet again, the direction of my life was to change. The advent of a new and younger headmaster, Stanley Crame, was like turning over another page for me. He loved gardening and nature studies, both of which I excelled at. He also kept bees and, after school, he sometimes allowed some of his pupils to help him with rudimentary beekeeping. Once I had become reasonably proficient he gave me two hives full of bees.

My stepfather was not best pleased about this, disliking the thought of having bees too near the house. So I was only allowed to accept them on the condition that I placed them as far away as possible, in a corner of one of our meadows. One day he fell asleep whilst sitting in the sun outside the front door and was stung. It could have been a bee from somewhere else of course but I wanted it to have been one of mine. He was not pleased and threatened me with the removal of the hives, an empty threat because there was no way he would ever get too close to them. I noticed though that he quite enjoyed the honey he spread on his toast at breakfast every day.

In the late 1940s and early 1950s the education system in Britain was going through radical changes. Secondary modern schools started to come into being for children over eleven who had not sat for and passed the eleven plus examination but, because this transition was in its early stages, my friends and I stayed on at Aldborough. I will never know what I missed by not going to a secondary modern school but I enjoyed my time at Aldborough and now believe that an upheaval at that time of my life may well have set me back.

After about a year at Meadow Farm I had come to know just what was expected of me and tempered my behaviour to suit. I suppose this was not such a bad thing for I became skilful in the art of judging the mood of others, something I have found beneficial in relationships ever since.

With hindsight I now realise that the excessive discipline brought to bear on me by my stepfather had its advantages. He ruled by fear and, frankly, at times was tyrannical. I have already mentioned some of the methods he used for obtaining obedience. He would tie me to my chair at meal times for not eating my food and I was forced to stay tied up until I had eaten every crumb. He did not hesitate to use his strap on me for only minor offences such as answering back or staying out late without a satisfactory excuse.

In those days it was not uncommon in farming households to have a double-barrelled twelve bore shotgun standing in the corner of the living room and, on more than one occasion, he threatened me with this. Once, as I fled from his anger into the small plantation of mature oaks close to the house, he actually fired a shot into the trees over my head. He also kept ponies that he broke in himself and these, too, were controlled by whips. Likewise he sometimes cracked a whip at me from time to time, just making contact with the knotted end. When this happened, especially if it caught my bare legs, it would bring up a red weal that stung like mad until it turned into a bruise.

For a long time I hated my new life and now and then, in sheer desperation, I would run away and hide in the nearby woodland, staying there as long as I dared, sometimes until well after dark. Eventually, of course, I had to pluck up the courage to return home to yet more punishment.

Mum always tried to protect me, often coming out of the house to meet me when I came home from school to warn me that Walter was in a bad mood. Although I never saw Walter actually abusing her physically, I was present on many occasions when he vilified her. Swearing was second nature to him and my poor mother always cowered and shrank back out of his reach.

Once every two or three weeks I was given an envelope of money and a parcel of meat, usually home cured pork from one of our pigs, and told to cycle to Felmingham with it in a bag hanging from my handlebars. My destination was to a local blacksmith who, in turn, gave me a parcel to take home. I never dared look but I got to know that it contained sugar, tea and other goodies not widely available in those days of rationing. I used to enjoy going to visit the blacksmith because he was a well-known speedway rider and he would often let me sit on one of the speedway bikes in his shed.

On one of these trips the blacksmith gave me a ten shilling note as change and to keep it safe I pushed it, folded, into the handlebar of my old bike. On arrival home I tried to remove the note which had become stuck, at first with my finger, then with a stick and finally with a piece of stiff wire, but succeeded only in pushing the note further and further up the handlebar. For fear of arousing too much suspicion I had to stop trying to retrieve the note and, foolishly, told my stepfather that I had lost it. This resulted in my receiving the usual punishment after which I was forced to retrace my journey, step by step, with the threat of another severe beating if I failed to find the money.

I knew of course that it couldn't be found but I hadn't the nerve to own up. For weeks afterwards I was treated like a pariah and only spoken to directly by my stepfather when he wanted to tell me off. Meanwhile the ten-shilling note remained firmly stuck in my handlebar. Eventually I plucked up the courage to tell Mum about it and she promptly explained the state of affairs to her brother, my Uncle

Walter, who devised a way of retrieving it with a fishhook fastened to a piece of stiff wire. The note recovered, I told my stepfather I had found it in a hedge by the side of the road on the way to Felmingham. He never did find out the real reason for its disappearance but I was pretty sure that he did not fully accept my explanation for its sudden return.

All this, sadly, paints a picture of my stepfather as a very miserable person who bullied his way through life at the expense of everyone else's feelings. In truth, the bulk of his bullying was aimed at me but I suppose that when I became a part of the family after Nan died, I must have been quite a handful, at least initially, and needed discipline. Furthermore, even though I was not aware then that I was not his son, he knew.

On the odd occasion he could be quite human and would tell my sister and me what we considered fascinating tales of his antics when a young man. He had been a farm worker and his stories mostly covered life on the farm and his relationship with his peers and some of his bosses. He had also been a poacher and he had many a tale about the 'cat and mouse' scenarios he played out with the gamekeepers and country policemen. On special occasions, when other members of his family came to visit, he would play his accordion, accompanied by his brother Bob playing spoons on his knee and one of his sisters, Christine, playing a harmonica. They played tunes such as 'If I Were a Blackbird', 'Somewhere over the Rainbow' and 'The White Cliffs of Dover'. On high days and holidays, especially at Christmas time, Walter would hang an apple from the centre of the room and, with our hands held behind our backs, we would play 'snap apple' – the object being to grab a big apple with our teeth.

As time wore on Walter's health started to deteriorate. He was asthmatic and had trouble breathing, so he spent his days and nights sitting in an old, well-padded armchair that had been raised above normal height with blocks of wood placed under the legs. I do not recall him ever going to bed.

For his condition the doctor prescribed a medicine called Felsol that had to be taken in powder form. This procedure was almost ritualistic. First the paper, containing each dose, had to be folded like a funnel, his head tilted back and the powder sucked in from the paper through pursed lips. This was always followed by a gulp of cold tea from a teacup always kept nearby on the mantelpiece. He also used an oral spray from time to time. Mum was not allowed to use any furniture polish or any household product that was in any way scented. Later, after I had left school, his illness worsened. Our doctor taught Mum how to inject Walter with, I believe, adrenaline. As time went on, the frequency of these injections increased.

All of this meant that I lacked any male influence in my life – at least, one that I could respect. When I was not doing chores I spent hours alone in my tiny bedroom at night, reading with the aid of a torch under the blankets or, at other times, out in the woodland that surrounded Buck Brigg. I did not find passing the time in this way a hardship for I had always found my own company agreeable, at least to the extent of never being bored with it. Throughout my formative years I spent hours cycling around North Norfolk to get away from the harsh regime of home. Usually on these trips I would take with me three of the popular little pocket-sized books from the Observer series Birds, Trees and Wild Flowers. From these books I learned to recognise many wild native species; knowledge I found very useful in later years

The little hamlet of Buck Brigg consisted of two smallholdings and a pair of semi-detached cottages. We lived in one of the smallholdings and the other housed the Bell family who used to hawk fish around the villages with a pony and trap. I never knew Mr Bell's first name because he was always known as 'Cockle'. As well as fish he sold cockles, mussels and Cromer crabs. He always cooked the crabs at home and I found it distressing to hear them screaming as they were dropped into boiling water to be cooked.

The two semi-detached cottages were the homes of the Fabb and Pull families. I met Gordon Fabb by chance one day when I was about ten and, as time went by, came to know him very well. In fact he became almost a substitute father. He had been a soldier in the Royal Norfolk Regiment. One of the battalions of the Royal Norfolks that had not gone to Singapore was based in India during the war and also saw service in Burma. Gordon's stories of army life fired my imagination, especially those of jungle warfare against the Japanese. Gordon owned a Velocette Viper motorcycle that I helped him clean from time to time. He took me for rides on the pillion and. later, after I had reached the age of seventeen, taught me to ride it. He was a keen football fan and occasionally would take me to watch Norwich City. I have been an ardent fan of the 'Canaries' ever since. He also introduced me to freshwater fishing and I spent many hours at this, sometimes with him but, mostly, alone. I loved the solitude and the feeling of being part of nature.

The occupants of the second cottage were, as I have said, the Pull family. I may have known Mr Pull's first name once but he was always called 'the accumulator man' and this is how I remember him. I had to take our accumulators to him to be charged every week. Accumulators preceded high-powered batteries for powering the wirelesses of those days. Because these glass containers were full of acid they had to be carried with the utmost caution.

Most of my angling was done at Gunton Lake, a large expanse of water in the Park that surrounds Gunton Hall, a large, rambling, old seventeenth-century house, then occupied by the Harbord family, descendants of Lord Suffield. By the 1940s the Gunton Estate had fallen on hard times but the opulence of the past was still evident from the collection of trees in the park, the large, derelict walled garden and a decrepit hunting lodge. This estate once owned all the land and houses of Buck Brigg. I understand that, up to the demise of the Suffield family, it sustained up to ten full-time gardeners and dozens of estate workers as well as numerous servants and farm workers, thus providing many jobs for the village and surrounding area.

Gunton Park has numerous chestnut trees and Mum, Rosie and I used to collect large quantities of the nuts every year. Some would be stored for Christmas and others roasted on the hob of the range in our living room, but I liked them best boiled, both hot and cold. This range was always alight, summer and winter. Apart from heating the house it was the only means of boiling water and cooking.

Right up to the time I was twelve, Saturday night was bath night for the family. Out came the deep galvanised tin bath, half filled with hot water from a large, long-handled iron saucepan boiled on the range and topped up with cold water from a bucket. Towels in readiness for drying were hung on the fireguard to warm and then we were bathed in turn. We were lathered with Sunlight soap and then rinsed off with water poured from a jug. Our hair was only washed every other week using the same soap, shampoo being too expensive. After a brisk rub down with a rough towel until we tingled all over, it was straight to bed. When we were safely tucked in it was the adults' turn for their weekly wash down. Once I reached thirteen we took it in turn to bathe in the privacy of the kitchen.

Fireguards were essential to prevent sparks leaping out on to the mat in front of the range. The staple fuel was logs, mostly sawn by me. Coal was used sparingly amongst the logs because it was very expensive and rationed. The fireside mats were known as 'piece mats', made by Mum from odds and ends of material collected from discarded clothes that Rosie and I had cut into 3 by 1 in. strips. These strips were then threaded with a special tool into a piece of sacking and out again, leaving a loop at the base and two projecting pieces that eventually formed the surface of the mat. Mum used to create patterns in the mats by using different coloured pieces. She made these mats in all sorts of different shapes and sizes and they were used throughout the house.

It was one of my tasks every evening after school in the autumn and winter to saw, with a hand-held bow saw, enough logs to last through the next day and night – about two heaped wheelbarrows full. These logs were usually sawn from wood collected by me from adjacent woodland and obtained by dragging dead or dying trees, sometimes for hundreds of yards, to the home-made sawing horse. Kindling wood to light the fires each morning also had to be collected from dry sticks and shoots lying about the wood and hedgerows.

As well as sawing wood when needed, I always spent a couple of hours doing compulsory chores every day after school. I had to collect the milk every day and this meant a walk of about one mile through meadows and woods to the dairy farm owned by the English family. The milk came straight from the cows in those days and, on occasion, I used to watch Mr English milking. Once or twice he allowed me to try my hand at pulling the teats, not as easy as it looks.

We had some goats and these were easier to milk and I often had to help my mother do so. I can still hear in my mind the distinctive squirting and tinkling sound of the milk hitting the bottom of the galvanised bucket used for this purpose. Mum often made butter from the goats' milk, all part of the self-sufficiency of the household at that time. As well as goats we kept lots of free-range chickens and bantams. We also had about ten pigs and it was one of my jobs to muck them out once every week. Two or three times a year a butcher would come and slaughter one of the pigs. He would also joint the meat for salting and storing in the larder. We always reared turkeys and cockerels for selling at Christmas and I helped to pluck them ready for the market.

All these animals were kept at Buck Brigg but Granddad Howes farmed about eighty acres of glebe land roughly three miles away in the village of Hanworth. He also rented a barn, cattleshed and stables from the church. On this little farm Granddad kept calves to be grown on to bullocks, a couple of sows to produce litters of piglets and a pair of handsome Shire horses. I realise now what a valuable experience it was, learning the rudiments of mixed farming. Granddad Howes, who was also called Walter, taught me a great deal and trusted me far more than my stepfather ever did.

In the spring my chores became much more garden related. Planting cabbage plants, sowing seeds of peas and beans and planting potatoes were tasks at which I soon became adept. In the summer I was expected to hoe and hand weed these and, in the autumn, to harvest the potatoes and prepare the land by digging it over ready for replanting the following spring. The job I hated most of all was digging a hole once a week in the corner of the nearby field, in which to empty the contents of the lavatory bucket. Another of my 'evening' jobs was to tear up newspaper into approximately 6 in. squares, to hang on a nail in the lavatory for use as toilet paper. Most of the time we used the *Eastern Daily Press* for this purpose. Rather dull reading for a boy of my age while sitting on the toilet but once a week I tore up the *News of the World*, a far more interesting read for a lad approaching puberty.

I was also expected to help on Granddad's smallholding from an early age, especially during the school holidays. In the spring it was 'chopping out' – a term for singling out sugar beet to about 6 in.

apart with a hoe. In summer it was standing up sheaves of corn and helping to bring the harvest in on a horse-drawn wagon. Finally, I helped to build the thatched straw stacks. These stacks provided the only means of storing corn to keep it dry until it was threshed. Threshing was one of my favourite jobs. This was done by outside contractors who would bring along a steam engine and the tackle to separate the corn from the straw. As the corn was shaken from a machine called a drum it was poured into large hessian sacks ready to be sold to the corn merchants. The chaff was also kept in large bags to form part of the winter diet for the cattle. The spent straw was used for animal bedding and was piled into a stack by a special elevator brought by the contractors.

Threshing was a labour-intensive occupation and I remember having to take sandwiches and a bottle of cold tea for my lunch. In my memory, even now, I can still smell the potent mixture of steam, oil and straw. I can feel the warmth of the sun on my back and hear the hissing and grunting of the steam engine as it turned the complicated flywheels and belts of the threshing tackle (in Norfolk parlance 'troshing tackle'). I suppose, if I'm honest, the real reason why I enjoyed it so much was because I felt so grown up, being treated by the threshing team as an equal.

When I was about thirteen I had a rather frightening experience. I was entrusted to ride Kitty, one of Granddad's Shire horses, to the farrier at the local blacksmith's for shoeing. There was no saddle to sit on, just a sack. After Granddad had given me a leg up, the horse, with me on her back, set off at a gentle plod to the smithy at Suffield, roughly two miles away. After about a quarter of a mile Kitty was startled by the noise of a tractor or some other machine backfiring as it started up in an adjacent field. Her gentle plod suddenly turned into a gallop and I had to hang on with both arms around her neck. The reins had been jerked out of my hands and were now out of reach so I had no way of stopping the galloping horse. All I could do was to hang on.

After a mile or so she slowed down, out of breath, and I was able to retrieve the reins and take control once again. On arrival at the smithy I was shaking like a leaf but nevertheless proud that I had managed to hang on. After the farrier had replaced Kitty's shoes he offered to give me a leg up for the return journey. Rather than lose face I let him do so and the horse and I set off. Thankfully, we arrived back at the stables without any further mishap but I learned later that a neighbour had witnessed my adventure, and, for a while, I was seen as a future Lester Piggott for staying on the horse's back as we sped at a gallop towards Suffield.

Although we called our home at Buck Brigg a house it was really a large bungalow with one bedroom and a living room at either end in the front. At the back of the house were two smaller bedrooms, one at each end and, between them, a central kitchen – that we called a scullery, as well as a small pantry. My immediate family occupied the bulk of the house and Granddad Howes had the living room and bedroom at the north end. In fact, I think he was the tenant and we all lived with him. All our meals were taken at Granddad's end of the house these, without exception, cooked by my mother. After meals we went back to our own part of the house, affording Granddad, who lived until he was well into his eighties, the privacy he apparently wanted.

Unaware at that time that Granddad Howes was not a blood relative, although it would not have mattered, I spent many hours, especially in winter talking to him or, more correctly, listening to him as he recounted tales from the Boer War and the First World War. He served in both as a soldier in the Horse Artillery ('Tillery' as he called it). He loved his wireless although he never listened to it during the day because that would have been 'a waste of time'. Immediately after the dinner table had been cleared in the evening he would turn it on and tune into the BBC Home Service and listen attentively until 10 pm when he would switch off, light his candle and go to bed. He loved such programmes as 'In Town Tonight', 'Down Your Way', 'Twenty Questions' and, of course, the 'Nine o'Clock News'.

As I have said before, I too had to take a lighted candle into my bedroom at bedtime, which, until I was fifteen, was always at 9 pm prompt. The candle had to be extinguished by 9.30 pm. By then I was always reading and at lights out it was time to switch on a battery torch and continue reading beneath the sheets. The rest of the family did not consider books important but I used to get books from the mobile library that called at school every week.

Granddad Howes was a handsome man and walked briskly for his age, his back ramrod straight. He always had a clay pipe in his mouth, even when he was riding his old, upright bike. He both smoked and chewed a tobacco called Churchman's Counter Shag. He loved growing all types of greens, root vegetables and salad and I used to help him from time to time. He took immense pride in perfectly straight rows with never a weed in sight. He didn't like growing flowers and considered them the province of my mother. He did have one rose though and every year, in June and early July, this rose would burst forth with hundreds of soft, pink, fragrant flowers. Although he did not know its name it was revered by Granddad and no one was allowed to cut a single bloom from it to take indoors. It was his pride and joy.

Much later I learned that the name of his rose was 'Maiden's Blush'. This same rose bush is still growing vigorously exactly where it was then. Indeed, I took the first budding eyes from this very plant when I started my nursery in 1968. It gives me great pleasure to know that every one of the plants of 'Maiden's Blush' we send out from the nursery, to destinations all over the world, are clones of the plant I knew as a small child.

From the age of about ten I was sent to Sunday school at the local Methodist chapel. My family was by no means religious, certainly not Methodists but I suspect they felt that I should go for appearance's sake. I quite enjoyed the company of the other children there. I continued to attend every Sunday until I was about fourteen. Towards the end of my time there I noticed how Janet, a local farmer's daughter, had suddenly become very pretty. I always tried to sit next to her in the pews and wanted so much to be able to get to know her. This was the very first time I had ever experienced such feelings for a girl, but I was far too shy to do anything about it. Eventually she left to go to boarding school. After her departure, although I still attended, I no longer enjoyed Sunday school.

4
Growing Up – A Bit

Iwas on my way home after Sunday school one day when Mr
Walpole, a chicken farmer who lived opposite the chapel, waylaid
me. He asked me if I would like to have a job on his farm on
Saturday mornings. By then I was thirteen and the thought of extra
pocket money sounded good. Getting permission from home was
easy when I told them that, for five hours, I would be paid the
princely sum of one pound but I was told that I would have to hand
over half of it towards my keep. The job was horrible. I had to
scrape trays full of fresh, smelly chickens' droppings into a wheel-
barrow and empty them onto a pile in the orchard. Once, in the
autumn, I picked up one of the windfall apples to eat. Mr Walpole
was watching me from behind the curtains and, when he saw me
doing this, he threatened me with the sack if I took any more. He
was a hard taskmaster without a shred of humour in his makeup.
He made sure that I earned every penny he paid me. I came to loathe
the man and the filthy working conditions. Several times I was on
the verge of walking out but, when I thought of the money I was
earning, I stuck out my chin and got on with the job. Later I learned
that several boys before me had not stayed in the job very long.

The extended Howes family was spread throughout the county of
Norfolk and with their patriarch living with us our house became a
meeting place for them. Being unaware at that time of the circumstances of my birth, I thought they were all relatives. Sunday was the
big day, the day when they would all descend on us for high tea,
which usually consisted of something hot cooked by my mother or,
if not, Cromer crabs followed by Mum's pastries and sponge cakes.
Home-made bread and home-made jam was also a favourite. The
jam I liked most was damson, complete with the stones, giving it a
nutty flavour. This same taste also applied to my mother's plum pies.
The children would play 'Rich man, poor man, beggar man, thief'

with the 'cobbles' as we called them. These were arranged around the edges of the plates and counted off accordingly. From time to time we would also indulge in flicking them at each other.

After tea there was always a lot of banter and joke-telling while the ladies did the washing up. Following on from this one of the party played an accordion to accompany a singsong. On warm summer evenings tables and chairs were taken outside on to the lawn and the fun and games went on well into the night, sometimes enhanced by alcohol in the form of elderberry or blackberry wine and home-made beer, again made by Mum. On one of these occasions one of the older cousins brought her new boyfriend along and he came to sit outside with us children while the washing up was being done. We had already noticed that he had trouble pronouncing his 'r's' so, mischievously, we engaged him in conversation. When he was asked about his job, he said, 'I have a factowy that makes infwa wed way appawatus.' Children can be very cruel at times.

Sometimes on those weekend afternoons Walter's younger sister Chrissie would let me tag along with her as she walked through the woods close to our house, gathering hazelnuts and chestnuts. On one of these occasions she showed me how to make an acorn popgun. These were popular at school and once I knew how to do it I made my own. My school chums and I competed with each other to make the gun with the loudest pop. To make a popgun you need a 6 in. length of elder wood, with its pith removed with a red-hot poker, to form the barrel of the gun. A hazel stick approximately 10 in. long and 1 in. thick then has to be whittled down to fit into the barrel to become the plunger. Ripe acorns freshly picked from the ground make up the ammunition. To operate the gun an acorn is inserted into one end of the barrel. The plunger is pushed forcibly into the other end in order to build up enough pressure to expel the acorn at speed, making a loud popping noise. I doubt if many children would know how to make one of these today. They are now relics of the past, discarded in favour of high tech toys.

Aldborough is a sizeable village situated about five miles from Buck Brigg. For hundreds of years a midsummer fair has been held on the green in the centre of this village. This started as a horse fair and, since both Granddad Howes and Walter had horses and ponies we were always taken to the fair by pony and trap. Horses as a mode of transport were on the wane by the mid 1940s and with many of the parents of our peers owning motor cars I was always rather embarrassed that we still used a pony and trap. Before I started my Saturday job and had money of my own, I was given pocket money to spend at the fair but never enough for more than two or three rides on the dodgems or swings and to buy some candy floss.

One year, about two years before I left school and prior to obtaining a Saturday job, I was allowed to cycle to Aldborough Fair on my own to meet up with friends. I soon realised however that they had more money than I did and I felt awkward and uncomfortable. The fact that I knew their parents were better off than mine did not help, so I decided to cycle home early. I thought the house would be empty but, to my surprise, a van belonging to a friend of the family was parked in our yard. I didn't give this a second thought but went into the house and, feeling 'grown up' decided to help myself to some beer.

It was at this point that I heard strange noises coming from Granddad's end of the house. Feeling a little nervous I tiptoed quietly through the scullery and peeped through the partly open door leading into the room in which we took our meals. To my horror I realised that this man and an older female cousin were actually doing IT there, on the mat. Petrified in case they heard me, I could not tear my eyes away. Of course I knew a little about the birds and bees, in theory, but this was the real thing. I thought the man was hurting her at first because she was making a lot of noise but I realised that in fact she was enjoying herself. I did not know what to do for the best. I wanted to stay and see more but I was scared at the thought of being discovered. If I moved they might hear me and then I'd be in real trouble; if I stayed, wow, it didn't bear thinking about. Panic won and I tiptoed back the way I had come and sought refuge in my bedroom next door.

Unfortunately my bedroom door creaked and the couple, now making less noise, heard me. Still only partially dressed, they emerged and came straight to my room. I was then quizzed as to exactly what and how much I had seen. When I confessed that I had actually witnessed what they had been doing I was sworn to secrecy, on my life, as both were married to other partners. Needless to say, this is the very first time I have related this story.

Rosie had asthma attacks from time to time and frequently had to miss school. Neither of us were allowed to bring friends home, Walter did not like the intrusion of outsiders. Nor were we allowed to play and have fun in the garden: fun equalled too much noise and he did not like noise. If I wanted to play football or cricket with my friends I either had to go to their houses or play on the meadow, well away from the house.

In the mid-1950s Walter bought an electricity generator and had it installed in one of the outhouses. The house was wired for electricity and, as far as lighting was concerned, we moved into a new era. Even so, I was never allowed to switch on my bedroom light for reading. I still had to manage with a candle and, after lights out, a torch. Heating the rest of the house was still by coal or log fires, with the cooking being done, as before, in the old black-leaded range oven.

As for water, the water mains were not connected to Buck Brigg until the early 1980s. Until then all the water was obtained from two sources, a well in the garden and from a delightful little stream that wended its way through one of our meadows. The well water was not the most palatable drink and was often cloudy. We only drank it after it had been boiled. Water for all other purposes such as washing up, bathing, and laundry etc had to be carried by me from the stream in two buckets, or pails, as we called them. Two pails, one in each hand, are far easier to carry than just one.

Water carrying was one of my more pleasant chores. The stream was about 200 yards from the house and was full of wild life including newts, sticklebacks, minnows and water beetles. Occasionally I would catch sight of an eel through the clear water wriggling its way along the bed of the stream. In spring and summer there were many different-coloured dragonflies darting to and fro amongst the reeds. I remember sitting on the bank, keeping perfectly still, watching a pair of kingfishers taking tiny little fish they had caught in the stream into a hole in the bank to feed their babies. As for trees, there was a predominance of alder and numerous pussy willows. Clumps of watercress grew further along the stream and sometimes I gathered bunches of this to take home.

The meadow through which the stream ran had probably been undisturbed, except for grazing, for hundreds of years. In the boggy parts near to the 'beck', as we called it, marsh marigolds, buttercups and wild mint thrived. Close to the trees, in spring, primroses and cowslips enjoyed the dappled shade. In the open areas of the meadow I can remember lady's smocks, ragged robin, plantain, daisies, dandelions and an abundance of both white- and pink-flowered clover. My sister and I spent hours searching for the elusive four-leaf clover, which of course we never found.

Lots of insects were attracted by this profusion of wild flowers. Bumblebees of all sizes buzzed around in the clover and, on the sunny days in summer, numerous colourful butterflies fluttered around. My favourite insects were the grasshoppers and crickets. I remember I used to touch them with a stick to see how far they could jump.

Although I had seldom been absent since attending Aldborough School, the winter of 1947 proved to be the exception. The snow came in mid-January and continued right through to the end of March. It was impossible to get through the little lanes around Buck Brigg until after the roads had been cleared by gangs of farm workers; we were cut off for at least two weeks. By then we had almost run out of food and coal. It was also, predictably, bitterly cold and both my hands and feet were sore with chilblains. Because my bedroom was situated on the north-eastern side of the house, it was particularly vulnerable to the cold and although I took a stone hot-water bottle to bed with me, it soon lost its warmth. Windowpanes became frosted and in the mornings even the contents of the chamber pot were frozen. The lavatory was outside in the garden so no one ventured out into the biting wind to use it. To keep us warm at night during this prolonged spell of bitter weather, overcoats and other garments were used as extra blankets. In daytime I kept myself warm by cutting down young trees in the nearby woods and sawing them into short lengths to take back home on my improvised sledge, a sheet of corrugated iron folded up at the front and pulled over the snow by a piece of rope.

While he was headmaster at Aldborough School, Stanley Crame introduced a house and prefect system and I became head boy of 'Green' house; then, in my last year, I was made head boy of the school. I found myself attracted to my opposite number, the head girl. We always tried to sit together at dinner times and exchange smiles across the classroom, but it never developed any further. I really loved school and I enjoyed almost every minute. My favourite subject was art, followed closely by history and I am still fascinated by times past. I also quite liked English and my favourite teacher, Mrs Hall, was probably responsible for this; spelling however was not my strong point and still isn't. I hated arithmetic and even today two and two often makes five for me.

In the early years at this school I was never given pocket money although, unknown to Walter, I sometimes received small handouts from Mum to buy an occasional ice cream from the Italian ice cream man who came to the school during break time once a week. Rationing was still in force and there were never any coupons to spare for life's little luxuries. All the time I was at this school I was, of course, growing and Mum made all my clothes, fashioning them from adults' cast-offs. She also knitted socks and jumpers. I had a jacket made to fit me from a grey/blue RAF tunic, the marks made by the original flashes on the sleeves still visible. I had to endure the occasional snigger from some of my classmates when I wore this jacket but I probably had the only garment with a designer label in the whole of the school!

Another little embarrassment came about because of my welling-ton boots. At one stage I only possessed one pair of shoes, which were kept for Sunday best, and a pair of plimsolls for games, so I had to wear the wellingtons to school. I wore short trousers until I was thirteen and the wellies chafed and chapped my legs just below the knee.

I said earlier that when I started my Saturday job at the chicken farm, I had to share my earnings with my mother. Mum didn't really want me to do this but Walter insisted, so from my one pound wages I had to put ten shillings towards the household budget. Even so, with ten shillings in my pocket every week I felt rich. This enabled me to buy a more up to date, second-hand bicycle from a local shop for three pounds, paying it off, including interest, over twenty weeks. On this, as well as occasionally cycling to and from school, I rode miles and miles around North Norfolk, mostly alone, going nowhere in particular, except at weekends when I usually visited school friends.

Before I bought my bike I either walked to school or caught the school bus. Mostly, I went by bus but on fine days in late summer and autumn I walked home, collecting rose hips from the hedgerows en route. There were hundreds and thousands of these dog rose hips on the hedges either side of the school lane and I collected bushels and bushels to be sent off by the school for the making of rose hip syrup. I can't remember exactly how much I was paid for these hips but it must have been enough to make it worthwhile getting my arms and legs scratched by the prickly bushes. The syrup of course was a valuable source of vitamin C both during the war and in the postwar period when citrus fruit from abroad was not freely available. I was given a teaspoonful of this tasty, sweet syrup every morning before going to school. The seeds from the rose hips made very good itching powder and me and my mates used to put handfuls down the backs of the girls' blouses for the fun of watching them squirm and being told off by the teacher for not keeping still in class.

At about the time I started to earn money on Saturdays, a new comic for boys came into being, the *Eagle*. One of its heroes was Dan Dare, a space traveller, and every schoolboy of that era, myself included, would eagerly wait each week for the next edition. Two other weekly publications I bought were the *Beano* and the *Dandy*, but my favourites were the *Hotspur*, the *Rover* and the *Champion*, all three crammed with adventure stories to feed my vivid imagination. Every week I read them all from cover to cover.

In 1951, my last year at school, I travelled out of Norfolk for the first time. The school had arranged a coach trip to the Festival of Britain in London, a celebration of all things British, highlighting how the country had overcome the devastation of the Second World War. Leading up to that day it was doubtful if I could go because of the cost, but somehow, with my meagre savings and contributions from uncles and aunts from the Beales side of the family, I managed it. After paying the fare I had a little left over to

[33]

spend on refreshments and suchlike. It was a good day out with much camaraderie aboard the coach and not a little fraternising with the girls. In those days it took four hours to travel to London from North Norfolk. On the homeward journey we had a singsong. We arrived home very late and I have to say I felt secretly proud to be British, not to mention feeling self-important from actually having visited London.

5

Out into the Big World

A few weeks before I left school I was lucky enough to get the promise of a job at the famous LeGrice Nurseries at North Walsham. Stanley Crame, the headmaster, had recommended me to Edward LeGrice to train as a nurseryman. I remember feeling very sad on my last day at school. I think I was in tears as I biked home and, even as I write, I can feel a little pang of nostalgia because, as I have said before, I really enjoyed my last year or two at school.

Options of careers for school leavers in rural North Norfolk in the early 1950s were limited to farm work or the building trade, especially for those such as myself with no academic qualifications. I sometimes wonder just how my life would have evolved if I'd become, say, a carpenter or a bricklayer. This said, I have a feeling that I would still have been drawn to the soil. Anyway I chose horticulture, despite the fact that it meant cycling five miles each way, to and from work every day. I did this for the first two years, winter and summer. When I reached seventeen I bought a second-hand motorcycle, a 350 cc Velocette, passing my test at the second attempt. Needless to say, as with my bicycle earlier, this had to be bought on hire purchase.

I can't remember exactly when I started to feel a little insecure, largely due to an identity crisis that came over me from time to time during my last year at school. These periodic bouts of anxiety lasted throughout my adolescence. Looking back, it was probably as much mild depression as anxiety or maybe it was a combination of both. These feelings sometimes lasted weeks at a time, weeks when I became very insular and did not really want to talk to anyone. While at school I could more or less hide these feelings but, underneath, I wanted to be alone and avoided contact with others as much as possible.

No one, not even my mother, had ever told me that I was illegitimate but I spent my six and a half years at Aldborough School answering to two surnames, Howes and Beales. At first I preferred to be called Howes because it was the name of my family. Slowly though, it dawned on me that my mother's maiden name was Beales and it seemed strange that no one else at school had a double identity like me. There was obviously something wrong somewhere. I lived with this confusion for a year or two, wondering if the term 'bastard' applied to me but I was unable to work up the courage to ask anyone outright to explain my double appellation. Mum must have had her own reasons for not telling me.

This recurrent state of confusion gave me a huge inferiority complex that still returns from time to time, I believe I am able to conceal it nowadays. These identity crises went on until well after I started work at LeGrice's where I discovered the truth the hard way. One of my fellow workers was my second cousin and one day, quite innocently, he let it slip in conversation that I had been born almost a year before my mother met Walter Howes. This revelation upset me and I found it humiliating that although I had not known about my illegitimacy before, apparently everyone else did. For a long time I felt conspicuous and wanted to hide away, for even in the 1950s illegitimacy was still frowned upon.

My thinking was still muddled and I desperately needed to know more. I loved my mother and did not want to ask her outright in case I upset her. Eventually I plucked up enough courage to ask my favourite aunt, Aunt Ethel, to tell me the truth. She started to cry and told me that she didn't know my real father's name, or where he came from. She thought that he was probably married.

Edward LeGrice was an excellent boss, firm but fair. I am convinced I was put to the test on my first day, being asked to weed a large patch of sweet briar seedlings. It was a very hot day in mid July and the weeds far outnumbered the prickly briars, then three to four feet tall. My arms and legs were badly scratched and by midday I had to fight against the urge to give up and cycle home but in spite of these and an aching back I somehow persevered. To this day, when I smell the scent of Sweet Briar it immediately brings back memories of that first day at work. I must have passed the test as, the following day, the foreman gave that particular job to someone else and gave me the less arduous task of helping with the stocktaking of the roses. Once I became accepted at LeGrice's I thoroughly enjoyed my work and even the twice-daily cycle ride in all weathers.

In spite of the fact that I was still bothered by the circumstances of my birth I realised that all of a sudden, through my job, I was being given an opportunity to build a career and make something of myself in my own right. If I applied myself and did well I could become my own man – I now had a purpose.

When I started work at LeGrice's there were already two other Peters employed there and, as is the wont of workmen, I was soon given a nickname, this for the second time in my life. For no apparent reason I became known as 'Rickie'. After a few months of doing general tasks I became an assistant to Bob Hicks, the head propagator at the Nursery. At that time LeGrice's grew a wide range of other nursery stock as well as roses. Working with Bob was very rewarding. He taught me how to make both hard and softwood cuttings of all types of shrubs and how to graft and bud fruit trees. I didn't become fully involved with rose growing until I was in the middle of my second year there.

Only too aware since joining the workforce just how lacking my formal education had been, I enrolled in two correspondence courses, English and Botany. Because of these courses I became rather a recluse, studying well into the night by candlelight; usually kneeling on the bedroom floor and using the bed as a desk. Occasionally I emerged from my studies to watch Norwich City play football. After some of the games my old school friends and I sometimes went to the pictures. I loved the Westerns best of all and still do to this day. On Sundays in winter I would often join my friends in kicking a ball about on Aldborough Green and, in the summertime, we played cricket. This was more for fun than serious sport but eventually these get-togethers petered out, as we all became engrossed in our various careers.

When I was finally moved from the propagation department to work with roses I found that at first I was not over-enamoured with them because they were very thorny. It was after all wintertime, their dormant season, but when later on in summer they came into flower in the field, I realised how very beautiful they were and that, with careful handling, I was able to avoid the thorns. My first task with the roses was helping to dig them from the field. In those days, with little or no mechanisation, most of the nursery tasks had to be done by hand. Digging up roses without damaging their roots was an acquired skill which took me several weeks to master.

The LeGrice Nurseries were famous for their roses and these were distributed throughout the British Isles by British Rail who in those days had an efficient parcel service that everyone used, including the Post Office. Each consignment was expertly packed in straw, itself a skill.

On the night of 31 January and the morning of 1 February 1953 a combination of very high tides and a bitterly cold north-easterly gale resulted in what are now known as 'the North Sea Floods'. Many sea defences were breached at various places along the East Anglian coast, resulting in extensive flooding. Lots of lives were lost and property washed away. Further high winds and tides were forecast for the next few days. The various local councils asked for volunteers to help restore the sea defences. Edward LeGrice answered this call by inviting the entire nursery staff to volunteer and all the volunteers were taken in the nursery lorry to one of the worst-affected villages, Sea Palling. Here, without warning, the sea had swept away a huge stretch of the sand dunes, which were part of the sea defences. Seven of the inhabitants of this village were drowned and The Lifeboat pub, which was only a short distance from the shore, was completely swept away by the huge waves. With hundreds of other volunteers we spent two days, in the teeth of the biting cold wind, filling sandbags in order to close the huge gap in the dunes as quickly as possible. Although we worked very hard I never before, or since, felt so frozen with cold.

Later on, in the spring of that year, I became Edward LeGrice's assistant, helping him with his quest for new varieties by means of hybridising. I found this whole process fascinating and learned much from simply observing what he was doing, and by writing the labels for each cross he made. All the bushes to be used for hybridising were grown in greenhouses and the whole process had to be finished by June in order to allow the hips containing seeds to ripen. Towards the end of my first season as the boss's assistant, I was allowed to practice hybridising on my own to gain experience for the next season when I would be permitted to make crosses.

There is no doubt in my mind that Edward LeGrice, in his own quiet way, made a big impression on my life. He was a marvellous tutor and was very influential in my development, both as a plantsman and, perhaps more importantly, as a person. He talked to me as we worked, not just about the job we were doing but all manner of other things from politics to philosophy. Much of what he said was absorbed by my very fertile young mind. He was deeply religious, a staunch Baptist, but although he touched on his beliefs occasionally he never rammed them down my throat.

When he was not talking to me Edward LeGrice would go about his work humming hymn tunes to himself, sometimes breaking into renditions of his favourites. Those were the days of Billy Graham, the American evangelist, but I declined an offer by the 'old man', as he was known to the staff behind his back, to go with him to listen to this famous preacher when he visited Norwich on one of his nationwide tours.

Another epithet of endearment by which Edward LeGrice was known was 'father', presumably because of his religious leanings. Anyway, quite apart from all this, I learned a great deal about breeding new roses from one of the world's experts of that time. He took me through every stage of the process from the initial selection of the parents to the first flowering of the seedlings out of doors in the trial beds. I am still very proud to have been associated with the breeding of some of LeGrice's masterpieces, in particular 'Allgold', the first ever unfading golden-yellow floribunda, and 'Lilac Charm' a delightful lilac-mauve, single floribunda.

Concerned by the fact that so few school leavers were taking up farm work and realising that, with the advent of machinery and chemicals, agriculture was becoming much more of a skill than hitherto, the then Ministry of Agriculture instigated an Apprenticeship Scheme for school leavers. When I heard about this I asked Edward LeGrice if I could apply through him to enrol as an apprentice. He readily agreed and proposed that another trainee working for him at that time should also enrol. Thus Arthur Clouting, who was a little younger than I was, and myself became the first ever horticultural apprentices in the UK. We enrolled in a fanfare of publicity and it was the first time ever that my picture appeared in the *Eastern Daily Press*.

Part of the syllabus of this scheme was to attend Norwich City College for one day each week to study of the theory of horticulture and botany. Once I had grown accustomed to this, I plucked up enough courage to ask one or other of the female students to come out with me. I was, however, extremely shy and linking arms and going to the pictures was as far as it ever went. In any case an apprentice's pay would not stretch too far.

It was a three-year apprenticeship and, as I was already seventeen when I started it, my obligation to do National Service at the age of eighteen had to be deferred until I was twenty. At the end of my first year as an apprentice I passed the examination for the Royal Horticultural Society's Certificate of Horticulture, the first step towards furthering my career. As previously mentioned, in my second year at LeGrice's I became more involved with roses than any of the other specialist areas of the nurseries and I became adept at most of the practices of rose growing. In consequence roses became my first love and have remained so ever since. I found their names fascinating and their history and evolution totally absorbing. I could not get enough of the subject. I bought rose books by mail order and could never pass a second-hand bookshop without going in to browse through the gardening section. I also joined the Royal National Rose Society; little dreaming that one day I would become its President.

All the books I collected I read avidly and the story of the rose, from its very beginnings, fascinated me. My imagination was stimulated by everything I read and absorbed; such as the mythical birth of the white rose. Apparently as Aphrodite was born, rising up from the sea, the droplets of water that fell from her turned into white roses. Later a jealous suitor, who had taken on the form of a wild boar, killed her lover Adonis. Aphrodite arrived on the scene just as he was dying and turned him into a red rose. I also came across Walter de la Mare's quotation 'Oh, no man knows through what wild centuries roves back the rose'. All this made me hungry to learn all I could of the progress of the rose through time. I discovered that the earliest reference to the Rose dates back to Homer's *Iliad* of the ninth century BC, when he tells that, to celebrate his victory over Hector, Achilles decorated his shield with roses and anointed Hector's body with rose oil. Moving on in time, the Egyptians, Greeks and Romans all adored roses. The Romans especially were infatuated by them believing that the rose possessed aphrodisiac qualities. They would carpet the floors of the banqueting halls with rose petals for festive occasions. They also planted them in greenhouses containing trenches that were kept filled with hot water by their slaves in order to provide blooms all the year round. Acres and acres of roses were grown in fields south of Rome to satisfy the incessant demand. After the decline of the Roman Empire, however, the popularity of the rose waned and through the Dark Ages and medieval times the Church rejected roses as they were thought to have become tainted by pagan cults and practices. It was not until the Middle Ages that the rose regained favour manifested by the many carvings depicting the rose in churches of the period. I was also fascinated by the fact that some of the damask roses we still have today were brought back from the Middle East by the Crusaders of the twelfth and thirteenth Centuries. The rose was also used extensively as a heraldic symbol and I will touch on this later on in the book, in the context of the Old Roses.

I very much liked the thought, too, that the love of the rose in ancient times extended to the Far East, especially China. Confucius wrote, in the fifth century BC, that a large number of roses had been planted in the gardens of the Imperial Palace in Peking and, although having to take third place to the peony and chrysanthemum, the rose was considered very important in the Ming Dynasty for its fragrance. The production of rose water was only permitted for personages of high standing in society. Commoners discovered wearing rose water would be severely punished. I think it is now generally known that many of our modern roses came about initially from the introduction of genes from China roses to our European native roses, the Chinas having been introduced to the West in the late 1700s.

One of the pluses of working for LeGrice's was being able to help at shows. At every show an apprentice would help stage the exhibit and sell the roses to the show visitors. In those days, except for Chelsea Flower Show when the roses were grown in greenhouses to force them to bloom early, the flowers were cut from the fields and packed into large boxes to be transported to the various venues.

During the summer there was a show every fortnight in the RHS Halls at Vincent Square, Westminster. We travelled from North Walsham to Liverpool Street Station by train and across London to the Halls by taxi. Once there the roses were arranged in bowls. We always exhibited about thirty different varieties on the stand, with thirty or so roses to each separate arrangement. These were then displayed on ready-prepared tabling of about a hundred square feet which first had to be covered with black cloth. The exhibits were always competitive, with rose nurseries from all around the country taking part. Our stand usually received a silver or silver gilt medal. It was never big enough to justify the award of a gold medal but we always took lots of orders.

Although each show lasted for two days we never stayed in hotels, which were considered too expensive. We always caught the tube to Sutton in Surrey to stay in bed and breakfast accommodation owned by one of the relatives of a member of LeGrice's staff. I have to say that I preferred arranging and staging the roses to actually taking orders for the bushes. As a country boy from Norfolk I was far too shy and lacking in confidence to feel comfortable talking to anyone with, as I thought then, a 'posh' accent. There is always a very distinctive smell in the RHS Halls when a rose show is being staged; the fragrance of the roses mingles with the smell of paint being used to titivate the staging props. Years later when I attended shows at the RHS Halls this smell never failed to evoke memories of showing for LeGrice's.

6

For Queen and Country

My apprenticeship seemed to fly by and one day in November 1956 I received my 'call up' papers. These instructed me to report to Magdalen Street, Norwich for a medical for my National Service. I passed the medical, was interviewed, then sat an intelligence test. After this I was asked which branch of the Services I would prefer. The Navy did not appeal to me but, in any case, I knew there were only limited vacancies for National Servicemen to become sailors. I realised that I didn't have a good enough education to become part of an aircrew in the RAF and had no desire to spend the next two years possibly sweeping out aircraft hangars; so I asked if I could join the Army.

Just before Christmas my enlistment papers arrived, in an official-looking Ministry of Defence manila envelope that I opened nervously, to discover that I was to make my way to Oswestry in Shropshire to become a soldier in the Royal Artillery. On 7 January 1957 I set off by train from Norwich to London where I caught a train to Oswestry. At Oswestry railway station literally hundreds of young men alighted from the train. I had met one or two of them on the journey and, as we were all going to the same place, a bond had already started to develop. It was comforting to realise that I was not on my own. Like me, they were all putting on a brave face. Most of us had never been away from home for any length of time before. At the station we were rounded up by a couple of sergeants from the barracks, herded like cattle into the back of army lorries and driven to our camp.

On arrival we were shepherded into squads of twenty or so, each squad being allocated a Nissen hut as their barrack room. Every hut was identical and we were told to select a bed, this to be our personal space for the duration of our two weeks' initial training at Oswestry. In the ablutions block there was only one toilet for twenty of us although there were three urinals and half a dozen or so wash-basins with mirrors for shaving. Strategically placed to serve about four huts was a shower block with about six showerheads fixed to the ceiling. I soon found out that there is no such word as 'modesty' in the Army.

On our first day we queued at the quartermaster's store to be issued with all the kit required to see us through our National Service, two of everything and one topcoat. To a large extent the sizes were guesswork. My two battledress blouses were far too big, but on my first leave a few months later my mother set about alter-ing them to fit me. The flannelette underpants and singlets, in a fetching shade of khaki, produced a few titters and the wags amongst us asked where they could pick up their carpet slippers and silk dressing gowns but were given short shrift with 'You're in the Army now'.

I was already getting to know the strict, orderly routine I would have to come to terms with. There was no choice: to go against the grain would be to make life hell. Even during the first few days any-one who rubbed the NCOs up the wrong way was punished by some means. Standing to attention without moving for two hours was a favourite way of bringing dissidents into line. Another was to be made to march at the double around the parade ground, in full view of anyone who passed, until ordered to stop.

Each of our barrack huts was arranged in such a way that a bom-bardier slept in one of the corner beds near the door with the sergeant's bed behind a partition in the opposite corner. The sergeant could keep an eye on us at all times through a window in this parti-tion. I was assigned to B Troop. It was our troop sergeant's job to give us our first grounding in square-bashing and to iron out the 'many wrinkles of our misspent youth', as he put it. He also instructed us on other aspects of soldiering such as how to walk briskly and upright, how to salute and, above all, how to make a blanket roll. This was a skill I found very difficult to master.

Every morning our troop commander would come into the hut to inspect our blanket rolls. If not up to standard he picked them up and scattered the blankets all over the floor. There was a rule that until our blanket rolls had passed muster we were not allowed to go to the cookhouse for breakfast. He seemed to single me out almost every day during those first two weeks, shouting 'Beales, you can do better', and threatening to return in ten minutes – which he always did. Because of this I sometimes missed breakfast altogether. When I moved on from Oswestry the part of 'soldiering' I could do best was to make a perfect blanket roll.

During those first two weeks we all had to have our hair cut short by the camp barber, known for some reason as 'the butcher'. Some of the young trainees were nearly in tears as their carefully groomed 'teddy-boy' and 'Tony Curtis' – otherwise 'D.A.s' (D.A. stood for 'duck's arse') – hairdos were shorn off to become even shorter than the regulation 'short back and sides'. We were taught both quick and slow marching with the correct swing of the arms and rifle drill with wooden replica guns. We were taught, too, how to bull our boots to the point of seeing our faces in the toecaps, blanco our belts and gaiters and iron our uniforms.

The days were long and when we had money we went to the NAAFI from 9 pm onwards to buy something to eat, perhaps a bacon sandwich. Woe betide anyone who was not in bed by 10 pm. We all came from different backgrounds in 'Civvy Street' and, without exception, the discipline was hard to take. In my intake alone two of the lads absconded, only to be picked up from their homes by the Military Police. I have no idea what their punishment was because they never came back. I imagine it was severe. They must have been very homesick indeed to have the courage actually to run away. In fact most of the trainees were very miserable and were missing their families.

The whole regime was quite a culture shock. In my case I didn't feel too bad for, in truth, I had just exchanged one set of disciplines for another. This said, I felt sorry for those who were upset, especially when I heard the muffled sobbing as one or other of my fellow recruits cried into his pillow in the dead of night. I suppose it was something to do with my not showing emotion, and perhaps because I was two years older than most of them, that I found myself being adopted by some of the lads as a sort of 'Dutch uncle'.

I had come from a fairly sheltered, rural background but I learned during those first two weeks at Oswestry that my fellow National

Servicemen came from all over Britain and their attitudes, values and backgrounds were very different from mine. Two of them were married and were the worst affected by homesickness. In my barrack room alone there were a couple of hard cases from the Gorbals in Glasgow who made life difficult for themselves by rebelling against any form of authority. There were two or three 'wide boys' from the East End of London who needed no prompting to become the proverbial 'barrack room lawyers' and two Liverpudlians who were always at each other's throats because one of them supported Everton football club and the other Liverpool. As for the rest, there was a coloured lad from Birmingham, several country boys like myself and a few who obviously came from good backgrounds, all thrown together by circumstance.

By the end of the second week most of us had mastered the basic practice of soldiering so, on the last day, we were told to pack our kitbags and report to the Main Square where transport was waiting to take us to Oswestry Station. We all assembled, each in our troop, and waited as our names were called in turn, according to where we had each been posted for the second part of training, this time for twelve weeks. After what seemed an age my name was called, prefixed by my Army number, 23361883 – a number I will never forget. I was posted to Tonfanau, an Artillery training camp overlooking Cardigan Bay in West Wales and given a railway pass to get there.

For some reason very few of my fellow trainees at Oswestry had received the same posting and I had a carriage to myself for one of the most picturesque train rides I had ever had, right through Snowdonia. The train stopped at every station from Oswestry to Dolgellau, where I had to change trains for Tywyn. At Tywyn I and a few other trainees from Oswestry, whom I had not come across before, were met by a bombardier to be taken the remaining three or four miles to Tonfanau in the back of a three-ton truck.

For the next twelve weeks I did not know what had hit me. It was absolute hell as far as discipline was concerned. I am sure all the NCOs and junior officers had been handpicked for their ability to give anyone beneath their rank a hard time, with new intake trainee gunners such as myself at the bottom of the pile. Soon after I arrived I learned that Tonfanau's nickname among the soldiers was 'Sheep

Shaggers' Creek', brought about by the fact that lots of sheep grazed inside the boundary of the camp. Trainees were not allowed out during their three months' training, not that there was anywhere to go in this remote God-forsaken place. In fact it seemed to me that the world outside had ceased to exist.

Gradually I adjusted to a more stringent set of disciplines, finding it easier to knuckle under than fight against them. Another qualification needed to be an NCO at Tonfanae was a very loud voice. On one occasion, having just had two teeth removed, I made the mistake of walking into the line of sight of the sergeant taking our troop for marching drill on the other side of the square. On seeing me, he bellowed my name at the top of his voice, ordering me to join the marching troop – 'AT THE DOUBLE'! When I removed the handkerchief from my face to explain that I had had two teeth removed he simply said 'Join the squad and get on with the drill.' Since the anaesthetic had already begun to wear off, I was in considerable pain and blood was pouring from my mouth, down my chin and on to my tunic. I just had to grin and bear it, not easy in the circumstances.

Quite apart from the bullying I also witnessed racism at Tonfanau. A few of the young National Servicemen of my intake were coloured and were subjected to even worse bullying by one or two of the more despicable NCOs as well as a few of their white fellow trainees. One or two of us made friends with a young lad of African descent in our barrack room but this was frowned upon by some of the more racist trainees and we were chastised for fraternising with 'that monkey'. This said, such was the demand on our time during training that it was almost impossible to cement any firm friendships. Reveille was at 6 am and lights out at 10 pm. So by eight in the evening, except for those who played poker, the best place to be for those last two hours was in bed reading, or writing letters home to mothers, wives or girlfriends.

The entire time at Tonfanau was designed to break us in as soldiers. We learned discipline by marching, rifle drill and cross-country running, not to mention all the time we spent in the gym doing pull-ups and press-ups and apparatus work. Another discipline was learning the drill necessary to deploy the Bofors L70 anti-aircraft gun. There is no doubt that by the end of our initial period of training we were far fitter than we were before we were called up. Although few of us would admit it, our minds were undoubtedly sharper and our reactions quicker. Two or three days before the end of our training at Tonfanau we were all mustered into the gym to receive our postings to the various Artillery regiments stationed around the world at that time. Our names were called alphabetically so I did not have to wait long to receive mine. I was posted to 22nd Anti-Aircraft Regiment, bound for Malta. I was thrilled and excited because it was an overseas posting and I had always wanted to see the world.

The British Army had a presence in many other countries besides Malta in the 1950s and I could have been posted to places as far apart as Malaya, Cyprus, Hong Kong and, of course, Germany – to name but a few. The regiment I was to join had been stationed in Germany until only recently and had moved to a transit camp at Shorncliffe, en route for Malta. The Suez crisis of 1956 had caused all sorts of political fallout, including the resignation of Sir Anthony Eden, the then Prime Minister. Most of the world powers disapproved of Britain's attempting to take the Suez Canal by force to thwart its nationalisation by Egypt. I recall listening to the news bulletins on the wireless just before I was called up and wondering if I might become embroiled in a Third World War, something that was not beyond the bounds of possibility at that time. In the end, with much loss of face, Eden gave in to the pressure, especially that of the Americans.

My initial training finished, it was handshakes all round and off on two weeks' embarkation leave. I felt very proud going home wearing my uniform for the first time outside the camp, despite its poor fit. Even my stepfather Walter seemed pleased to see me and I was to discover that he had mellowed considerably in my absence. To use up my time whilst on leave I helped on the farm with such things as cutting hedges and digging the garden. It was good that I was able to talk to the newly reformed Walter almost as an equal – almost, because I still harboured memories of his former harsh treatment. In the meantime my mother found time to set about altering my uniform to make it a better fit.

Before I left Tonfanau to go on leave, I was issued with passes to take me by train to Napier Barracks, Shorncliffe, Kent the then Headquarters of 22nd Anti-Aircraft Regiment. However, to my great disappointment, three days before my leave was due to end, I received a telegram informing me that the regiment's move to Malta had been cancelled, but I was to report to Napier Barracks anyway. I surmised that it was probably for political reasons that 22nd Ack-Ack Regiment RA was not sent to Malta. It would have seemed, to both our allies and enemies alike, as too much sabre-rattling. In the event, the regiment just had to hang on at Shorncliffe, waiting for somewhere to go.

After about six weeks the majority of the regiment moved, in convoy, to Llanion Barracks, Pembroke Dock, South West Wales. My battery however was sent to London to act as support to the participants in the Royal Tournament, a military tattoo held at Earls Court. Some of us did mundane duties such as simply showing the audience to their seats. Others, including myself, were designated to let off fireworks behind the scenes in support of some of the demonstrations of gunnery and warfare of all types.

These duties lasted just two weeks, then it was off to Pembroke Dock, South Wales to rejoin the regiment. By now I had become accustomed to being a soldier and, soon after arriving at Llanion Barracks, I became part of D Troop, 53 Louisberg Battery and became a member of one of the gun crews. Each Bofors L70 had five operatives – No 1, the NCO, in charge; No 2, which was me, being the gun layer; and the three other gun crew loaded and handled the ammunition. After a short spell learning the basics of gunnery each troop, in turn, went to Manorbier Camp for firing practice, shooting at a drogue pulled by a small plane, out over the Bristol Channel. I fired twice, missing both times. It would have been a miracle if I had scored a hit at that time, or so I heard, as very few National Servicemen had ever succeeded in doing so. Ammunition was too expensive to allow us to fire more than two rounds of live shells during any one deployment.

After some three months of gunnery training I was offered the job of becoming driver to the battery commander, Captain Martin Farndale, a job I accepted with some trepidation for I still had the countryman's respect for the officer classes. However, driving for Captain Farndale did me a very good turn, for such were his man management skills that I was soon able to talk to him on almost equal terms. Farndale was highly respected by the men of all ranks in the regiment and, as the driver of his Champ, I was the envy of many. The Champ is an amphibious vehicle, although I was never called upon to drive it through water. It was a super little 4 x 4. Some years later, long after National Service, I heard that the Army had taken the Champ out of service, replacing it with the Land Rover. I know not why; perhaps it was too expensive as it had a very powerful Rolls-Royce engine. Today it would be called a 'gas-guzzler'.

To my dismay, after only a short time as Captain Farndale's driver, he was promoted to major and moved on to pastures new. I was not at all surprised to hear, many years later, that he had moved up through the ranks to become Master Gunner, the highest rank in the Royal Artillery. As a field marshal, he ended his service as Commander in Chief of the British Army on the Rhine. I have to say that Farndale probably influenced my life at that time far more than anyone else I had ever rubbed shoulders with in the Army. Most of all, I learned how to handle men. I like to think that, even now, I still practise some of his invaluable techniques in running my own business.

Almost immediately after handing back my Champ, I became aware of a vacancy for a dispatch rider at Battery Headquarters. I ignored the old army adage about never volunteering for anything, so I asked, and got the job. Once again I had fallen on my feet for I loved riding motorbikes and, to all intents and purposes, I was almost my own boss, escorting convoys and running errands from camp to camp. Two or three times each year the regiment would go on manoeuvres at either Castlemartin Ranges or Sennybridge Battle Area. I enjoyed these as it often meant riding my bike over rough terrain.

In February 1958 the whole of 22nd Regiment RA was posted to Snowdonia for six weeks to clear the mountains and valleys of unexploded artillery shells from the days when it was a firing range. A necessity to enable the area to become the National Park it is now.

It was bitterly cold in those snow-capped mountains and although we all wore greatcoats, our clothing was not really designed for those conditions. As one would expect from the Army there was little sympathy for those of us who could not stand the cold. As a hardened countryman, used to working outdoors, I coped with it better than most. To me the weather was far less of a hardship than the dreadful mutton stew we had to eat every day. A three-ton truck would bring our lunch as near as it could to us and we would stand in line for a dollop from a ladle, served by an army cook. There was never any change of menu. Even as I write, I recall the stew's greasy consistency and unpalatable flavour but it was that or nothing and I had to eat! In order to force it down I used to swallow it without chewing, trying to pretend it was something more to my taste.

To clear the shells each troop took a section of the mountainside and spread out, each man about ten yards apart, walking in line abreast over the allocated area. If anyone found a shell he had to shout 'Shell' at the top of his voice and the whole line had to stand still and wait for it to be marked, both in situation with a flag and with a cross on an Ordnance Survey map. Only on the word 'Go' from an NCO could we move on. Later, the shells were disarmed or exploded by a bomb disposal unit. To occupy our minds during these searches the whole line of two hundred or so soldiers sometimes burst into song. On the coldest days the favourite ditty was a line from the Walls Ice Cream television advert: 'It's time we had a Walls ice cream, a Walls ice cream' and so on, ad infinitum.

Our billets for this exercise were Nissen huts at Trawsfynydd Camp. The work was very tiring. A few of the soldiers in my hut always played cards deep into the night, keeping me and others awake, but our protests fell on deaf ears. This meant that by my weekly day off I was usually desperately tired and spent most of the day fast asleep on my bed. Occasionally a duty sergeant opened the door and bellowed at the top of his voice 'Stand by your beds.' Shocked into sudden wakefulness, I leapt out of bed and did as ordered, only to find that he had done it just for the hell of it.

When our six weeks' spell of duty on the mountains ended, another regiment took over and I returned to my dispatch riding again. My first task was to help escort the regimental convoy back through Wales to our barracks at Pembroke Dock. Because by now I was so very tired from being kept awake night after night by my roommates playing poker, I fell asleep whilst riding my bike and ended up entangled in a very thick Welsh hedgerow. Luckily I wasn't hurt, except for my dignity As the convoy went past, one of the officers laughed and shouted, 'What are you doing in that hedge, soldier? No one ordered you to take cover!'

Throughout my National Service my mother used to send me food parcels. She was a good cook and knew that I had a weakness for her shortcakes. She also sent me another of my favourites, digestive biscuits. These usually arrived, through the post, as a packet of crumbs that could only be eaten with a spoon.

The 22nd Regiment was a part of the Second Army Group Royal Artillery and the Group's flash, worn on our sleeves, was a white circle with two horns set on a black background, representing Taurus the bull and known affectionately by the soldiers as 'the flying arsehole'. Along with all the other insignia, we had to sew them on to our uniforms ourselves.

Many a strong friendship was cemented during National Service. Les Lee, in particular, an Essex man fom Brentwood, was a close friend since we first met as soldiers. Sadly he died recently. Once, when we had a forty-eight-hour pass, he took me home to meet his parents. I first met Les, who was a three-year regular soldier and already a bombardier, in the junior NCOs' mess at Llanion Barracks after I had been promoted to lance bombardier. Most Saturday evenings we could be found in the town of Pembroke Dock, sometimes playing darts or simply having a drink in one of the many pubs. From time to time we went to the town's dance hall. This was one of the few places where soldiers could fraternise with the local girls. Rock and roll was then the in thing and many a romance started at these dances. There was one other venue popular with the local teenagers and soldiers alike, a coffee bar cum ice cream parlour called Monti's. This café had a jukebox and one could sit for a whole evening drinking coffee, playing the jukebox and chatting up the girls for very little outlay.

After an enjoyable time at the café one evening, my friends and I were making our way back to the barracks when we caught up with two girls. One of them asked us if we had any change for the telephone. She was an attractive brunette but my eyes were drawn to her blonde companion. Later I learned that her name was Joan. My mates were chatting up the brunette, so summoning all my nerve I asked Joan if I could walk her home. To my delight she shyly said yes. Soon we were seeing each other whenever possible and, after three months, became engaged.

One evening we were sitting at one of our favourite places, on Llanreath beach enjoying a beautiful sunset over Milford Haven estuary. It was high tide and there was a warm westerly wind bringing in the rollers which we could hear breaking against the rocks along the shoreline. On a sudden impulse I said to Joan 'If you were older I would ask you to marry me.' She answered 'Why don't you ask me anyway?' We are still together some forty-eight years later.

The next morning I woke up wondering how I could possibly afford to buy a ring, now that we were engaged. Army pay would not stretch to the sort of ring I had in mind. Apart from a few pounds in the Post Office Savings Bank, all I had of any value was my motorbike. I immediately wrote to my mother asking her to advertise the bike and sell it for me. It was sold within the week and the money was on its way to me shortly afterwards.

Now that we were to be married one day everything should have been straightforward but I still had my illegitimacy lurking in the back of my mind. I knew that I would have to come clean and tell Joan about it. One day, while we were walking on the beautiful beach at Freshwater West, I plucked up the nerve to tell her. It was not easy because I didn't know how she would react and also I felt guilty for not telling her earlier. Joan has since told me that she was concerned about what I was going to say because I looked so very serious. When I finally managed to tell her I was illegitimate she smiled and said 'Is that all? I thought you were going to say you had murdered someone.' I was very relieved at her reply because, until then, I had never actually told anyone outside my family. Later, when I was back at the barracks and in bed, it dawned on me that perhaps being illegitimate was not as black as I had made it out to be in my mind. Furthermore, I had no need to feel guilty.

I must say that Joan's family made me very welcome. They lived on the outskirts of Pembroke Dock and their house became almost a second home to me. It was good to become part of a family that was more relaxed than the one I was used to back home in Norfolk. Living at home with Joan were her father, her mother and her two siblings, Christine some six years younger than Joan and Phillip, two years younger still. Joan was born at the beginning of the Second World War and Christine at the end. Her father Albert was employed at that time in the building trade and her mum Freda worked as a cook in a café in Tenby, some ten miles away. Both her parents had been in the hotel industry when they first met, working as a waiter and waitress. They had both worked in large hotels all over the country prior to being married and setting up home in Wales. Joan's father was English and came from Worcester.

Freda, was quite a character, short, round and very Welsh. She was full of tales of folklore and ghosts and would recount stories of her childhood. She was the second child and eldest daughter of a family of seven, all born and brought up in Monkton, a village just outside the town of Pembroke, some three miles or so from Pembroke Dock. Freda's father had died of lung disease when she was in her teens, possibly from substances he had inhaled in the course of his work in the dockyard. Consequently she had to leave school and go into service. Her first job did not last long – as she explained: 'The lady of the house considered herself frightfully posh. When the coalman came with the coal delivery she would not let him take it through her clean house in his filthy boots and made him empty the sacks in the front porch. When he'd gone she said to me, "Now Mary" (she did not like my name) "get a bucket or something and carry the coal through the scullery to the coal shed."' At this point Freda laughed and said 'Who did she think I was? I just looked at her and said politely, "I'm sorry, ma'am, but I was employed as a housemaid not a donkey to cart coal. You'd better do it yourself."' 'Then', said Freda, grinning at the memory, 'I took off my pinny and that ridiculous cap and went home.'

Sometimes when we were on our own, Joan's father reminisced about his days as a gunner on the merchant ships, where he saw action in the convoys heading for Russia from America through the treacherous North Atlantic during the Second World War.

Joan's sister Christine and her brother Phillip were, of course, still at school then. As I said earlier, they all made me very welcome and accepted me into the family with open arms. Joan's mum and dad threw a lovely party for us on the day we celebrated our engagement. I invited some friends from the barracks and Joan invited some of hers. It was a good evening.

At that time Joan had just begun a pre-training course to become a state registered nurse at Glangwili Hospital in Carmarthenshire. We knew that once I was demobbed it would be very difficult to sustain our relationship from a distance so we had to make choices. I could have remained in Pembrokeshire but opportunities for employment were scarce in that part of Wales; certainly there was no work for a rose grower.

I had enjoyed my National Service so there was a strong temptation to stay on in the Army and become a regular soldier; but there was no guarantee that I would be able to stay in Pembrokeshire. In the end, with some temerity, I applied for a job working for Graham Stuart Thomas at Hilling's Nursery, Chobham, in Surrey. I had always held Thomas in high esteem and if I were successful it would be a wonderful opportunity to further my career with one of the world's leading rosarians. Joan, having left Glangwili Hospital, was accepted as a student nurse at Central Middlesex Hospital on the outskirts of London and, to my delight. I got the job at Hilling's and was due to start there after I was demobbed. Joan would also begin her training in London in January 1959. In the interim she took a job as a chambermaid in one of the local coastal hotels, Pembrokeshire being a popular location for tourists.

Towards the end of my National Service we were separated anyway because, for some reason I never quite understood, I was one of only a few National Servicemen from our regiment to be selected for the Army Emergency Reserve. This meant that, immediately prior to my demob, I had to go for four weeks' intensive training at a military establishment at Epsom in Surrey, there to be taught all sorts of different skills about rescue in urban situations. After about two weeks I managed to crush one of my fingers between a fulcrum and a brick and had to become a 'pretend' casualty for the remainder of the course. I must admit that it was somewhat hair-raising being strapped to a ladder and lowered down several storeys, pretending to be unconscious. I confess that I have forgotten much of what I learned on the course now but I am sure the idea behind this Emergency Reserve was sound.

By now the threat of a Third World War was hanging over the Western world. The theory was that, in the event of an invasion or the dropping of an atomic bomb on London or Manchester say, and assuming there was some prior warning of this event, the Emergency Reserve would be taken out to a remote island until it was all over. The Reservists would then be flown back to rescue any casualties and mop up the mess. I remained on the Reserve list for three years after leaving the Army.

7

Back to 'Civvy Street'

I had to return to Pembroke Dock for my official demobilisation and passing-out parade. A few days later Joan and I started a new chapter in our lives, Joan as a student nurse and myself at the Rose Department of Hilling's Nurseries, Chobham, Surrey.

But there was a cloud on our horizon because we could not see each other very often. Joan's hospital was on the northern outskirts of London and I was in Surrey. To see each other meant a bus ride to Woking Station or, from Joan's end, a tube journey to Waterloo Station, then half an hour by train and then another bus ride. The whole journey took about one and a half hours. Since Joan had only one full day off per week, a different day every week, it meant that we could only see each other once every two weeks or so, if that.

Joan lived in the nurses' home at her training hospital and I was fortunate to find lodgings with an elderly couple, Mr and Mrs Stevens in West End (the next village to Chobham). Jessie Stevens, the husband, had been a cook in a boarding school and still did the cooking in the household. The food was good, a definite plus. However, when I became their lodger I was not aware that Mr and Mrs Stevens were really looking for a substitute son. They had been foster parents for many years and obviously missed having someone to care for. In my eagerness to please and be accepted I fell into the trap and became almost one of the family. This of course made it rather difficult to escape their possessive cosseting. In order to keep them at arm's length I often visited the local pubs in Chobham and West End.

Meanwhile I was settling in at my new job as rose foreman at Hilling's which was then probably the biggest wholesale mixed hardwood nursery in the country. The rose department in those days was run by Graham Stuart Thomas, the author of two important books on roses, one of which was *Old Garden Roses*. It was these roses in which the nursery specialised. Thomas had built up a large, refined collection and they were slowly becoming a cult attraction. One day, without warning, after I had been working there about a year, Thomas suddenly announced that he was leaving Hilling's to become a director at Sunningdale Nurseries, just down the road from Chobham. Tom Hilling, owner of the nursery, asked me if I would take over the collection and move it on commercially; and so I became custodian of one of the most comprehensive and prestigious collections of Old Garden roses ever to exist until then.

During the short time I worked under Thomas I learned to respect his in-depth knowledge of the older roses. I also soon realised that he did not suffer fools gladly. His sense of humour was highly refined and he had no time for flippancy or half measures. Everything had to be just right for him and you could be sure that any statement of fact he uttered or wrote had been researched thoroughly and double-checked for authenticity. He learned his gardening skills and love of botany in his youth as a student at Cambridge Botanical Gardens. Later, following on from Hilling's, Chobham, and a spell as a director of Sunningdale Nurseries, Windlesham, he became Garden Advisor to the National Trust, a position he held for several years until his retirement. There are several National Trust properties in Norfolk, amongst them Blickling, Felbrigg and Oxburgh Halls, so whenever his job brought him into the vicinity of our nurseries he would call and see us. On one of these occasions he brought me budwood of one of his most important rediscoveries, the true form of *Rosa moschata*, which he asked me to distribute for him. Until he found the true form of this species growing in a garden in Essex, all known commercial stock worldwide had been confused. Likewise, he also sorted out the confusion between *R. longicuspis* and *R. mulliganii* but now is not the time or place to go into this in detail. Suffice to say that when Graham Thomas expressed an opinion on these matters, woe betide anyone who challenged it.

During the early years of his retirement Thomas took a keen interest in the famous rose collection at Sangerhausen, East Germany, which at that time, because of the Iron Curtain, was not easy to access. He started a correspondence with the then curator and somehow managed to persuade him to send budwood of many old varieties to England for propagation. He then asked me if I would bud these for him and grow them on at my nurseries. Many of the varieties he received from this source had been lost to the West. This went on for about three years and each summer he would travel up to Norfolk to inspect the latest imports. Armed with lots of old books, we would check them for authenticity together. We learned however not to trust the names on the plants, for years of neglect at Sangerhausen had resulted in many of the varieties having their labels muddled up, presumably by unskilled East German gardeners. At least fifty per cent of the roses imported by Thomas at that time were clearly wrongly named. From my nursery at Swardeston each batch of bushes would be sent to Castle Howard, Yorkshire, where they underwent further scrutiny by Jim Russell, the curator. He sifted out the errant varieties and planted out the authentic ones into display beds. Unless we could name any of the unknowns, they were destroyed for fear of adding further to the already confused nomenclature of the ever-increasing number of unidentified old varieties. In any case, who can be sure that any rose that predates human memory is correctly named? Like Thomas and Russell I believe that it is more important to have worldwide acceptance of a name of certain authenticity. This said, there are too many people in the rose world today who believe only what they want to believe!

Graham Stuart Thomas passed away in 2004 and, in my opinion, no other man has left such an indelible mark on roses from the past as he has. I feel very proud to have been given the honour of reading the lesson at his memorial service held later that year in Westminster, London.

I became besotted by the older roses after reading Thomas's books and, quite apart from appreciating their value as roses within the garden landscape, I loved the romance and heritage they represented as part of history through the ages. The collection I had taken over consisted of varieties and types of roses dating back to before the tenth century and had been collected by him from all over the world. One of the most famous of the tenth century roses is the pink and white Gallica 'Rosa Mundi'. One of the legends surrounding its origin suggests that it was named by Henry II after one of his mistresses, Fair Rosamund Clifford, an unlikely story I feel that came about by someone finding a plant of 'Rosa Mundi' growing near her grave. I believe it is more likely that the rose acquired its name as being 'The Rose of the World'.

Two other very famous roses in Thomas's collection that I came to know well are *Rosa gallica Officinalis* and 'Alba Maxima'. The former, 'The Red Rose of Lancaster', was adopted as the emblem of the Lancastrians at the time of the Wars of the Roses, the latter is thought to be 'The White Rose of York'. The Civil Wars were ended when King Henry II married Elizabeth of York in 1485. In our rose gardens we have planted a bed of 'The Red Rose of Lancaster' mixed with 'The White Rose of York', and they seem to be living together in total harmony.

The evolution of roses began with the pure roses of nature long before man intervened in their development. Man's intervention coincided with the increasing interest in gardening and the emergence of one or two specialist rose nurseries, particularly in France. By the time of Empress Josephine the rose had become very fashionable and multifarious new varieties started to be introduced. Josephine herself had a magnificent collection of Gallica roses in her gardens at Malmaison. She loved roses and during Napoleon's many absences spent a lot of her time overseeing her gardeners as they tended them. Her patronage of nurseries at that time inspired breeders to explore the wider possibilities of roses as garden plants, as well as constantly seeking to breed roses with bigger and better blooms for exhibition at garden shows, shows that were becoming more and more popular as time went on.

It was not until about the beginning of the Victorian era that the British took over from the French as leaders in the world of rose breeding and became pre-eminent at using roses in the garden landscape. During the following hundred years thousands of new roses were introduced, some of them vulgar and not deserving of staying the course, consequently falling by the wayside. One of the most attractive features of the Victorian roses was their perfume. Throughout that era roses were segregated into their own space within the garden and usually planted in formal beds of mixed varieties. It was not until the early part of the twentieth century that influential garden designers such as Gertrude Jekyll recognised the full potential of many types of roses. They began to use them more in supporting roles, combining them with other plants and giving them architectural roles on buildings and garden structures such as arches and obelisks. I have always been a follower of the Jekyll principles in garden design and wherever it is appropriate I try to incorporate them into my own designs, especially bringing the third dimension into play by using climbers and ramblers on some of the modern structures available to me today.

Although I had taken on the responsibility of Thomas's Collection, this was not reflected in my pay, which was meagre – just a fraction above the agricultural rate for a skilled nursery worker. With Joan's pay as a student nurse even less, we could not afford to see each very often and we found it very hard. Sometimes I would make the journey to North London and sometimes Joan would come to Surrey. My landlady understood and allowed Joan to stay over, whenever possible, sleeping in my room while I slept on the living room couch. This meant we could see each other a little more often but this was far from an ideal arrangement because our days off seldom coincided.

Eventually, after enduring two whole years of this, Joan decided to cut her training short and get a job nearer me. As she said, she had no particular desire to climb through the ranks to become a hospital matron, so it made sense. Neither did she fancy continuing her training at a Surrey hospital, so she applied and was accepted for a live in position as a nursing assistant in a private nursing home in Woking.

This was great because it meant we could see quite a lot of each other again and begin saving and planning for our wedding. After a while I realised Joan was unhappy and when I asked her why it all came out. She explained that the owners of the nursing home lived in Guildford, some miles away and they had installed an SRN as resident sister-in-charge. The sister and the other staff were very nice and the patients were, in the main, lovely but being privately owned it was all about money. If, as a patient, you had money, it was fine and you could have a private room and all the facilities. If on the other hand all you had was an old age pension book, tough – into a communal ward with no privacy at all. The draw sheets from this ward were washed on site and hung in the laundry room to dry, with the result that they became as stiff as cardboard and were of a dingy grey colour. Joan found all this very upsetting and resolved to find a more rewarding position.

One day an old gentleman was admitted to the nursing home. Unable to return home where he lived alone, having spent some time in hospital after a severe heart attack, he was forced to take up residence at the nursing home. It did not take him long to ask Joan to come and live in his house so that he could have someone in attendance at night as per the doctor's orders. Joan was undecided, would it work out? She would still need to get another job and even if she did get a better job, suppose she and her patient could not get on. It would mean she would be left with nowhere to live.

After a lot of thought she came to the conclusion that she really could not tolerate for much longer the conditions in which the poorer patients lived, so she decided to throw caution to the wind and accept the old man's offer. She need not have worried. Mr Orchard (we never knew his first name) was a real old-fashioned gentleman, impeccably mannered and very, very kind. He was in his mid seventies when Joan met him and a bachelor, having looked after both his parents until they died. He was very high up in Freemasonry and had been engaged for over twenty years to a lady who lived about thirty or so miles away, nearer London. She, too, had cared for both her parents until they passed away.

Meanwhile Joan had taken a position as a factory nurse in the medical department of James Walker Lion Works at Woking, a large engineering company. This meant that her salary was higher and, in spite of having to do a different shift each week, the working conditions were much better and there was a wider variety of nursing tasks. Much effort was centred on preventative medicine and health and safety throughout the factory. A visiting doctor came in three times a week to hold a surgery for the employees and Joan found it all very fulfilling.

Joan soon discovered that living with Mr Orchard was not at all difficult. At first he insisted that he would prepare the evening meal each day because, as he put it, 'You have to go to work.' After managing to force down three consecutive evening meals of lamb chop (with mint sauce), boiled potatoes and green peas followed by ice cream or fruit, Joan persuaded him that it would be much better for her to do the cooking since she could call in at the shops as she cycled home. This plan worked out well. Joan and I managed to see each other several times a week and I would always have to accompany her indoors to say goodnight to Mr Orchard, whereupon he would insist that we each had a small glass of very sweet sherry.

While all this was happening in Joan's life I continued lodging with the Stevenses and, because she now lived much nearer, I bought a very old 500 cc Triumph Twin motorbike from Joan's uncle, who lived on the other side of Surrey in Oxted. It was actually a prewar model with girder forks but it went like the wind. This old bike helped us to regain some sort of social life, visiting Joan's Uncle John and Auntie Vera at least once a month. I had also made friends with one or two of my colleagues at work, so from time to time we would visit a pub with them. Joan also had a special friend, Pam, who worked in the medical department with her, and we frequently went out as a foursome with her and her husband John.

After Joan had lived with Mr Orchard for about three months he suffered another heart attack, this one very serious, and had to be rushed into hospital where, sadly, he passed away a few weeks later. Joan was allowed to stay on living in his house. All this happened in the mid-summer and, earlier, we had set the date for our wedding for September, having previously arranged with Mr Orchard that we could live in part of his house (which was in West Byfleet), in exchange for Joan looking after him. His death upset our plans, but his relatives allowed us to get married from the house and continue to live there until we could find somewhere else.

All this suited us as by now I had rented some land at Pirbright, about eight miles from West Byfleet, and had started to grow a few roses there. The rose market seemed insatiable in those days, the late 1950s and early 1960s. British gardeners were just getting their appetite back for ornamentals after spending most of the 1940s growing only vegetables. Anyway it was not uncommon for nursery workers to grow a few plants on the side, so to speak, in their own gardens to supplement their rather meagre wages. In my case though, I was rather more ambitious with my own moonlighting activities serving the cause of starting my own rose nursery in the future.

We were married at Old Woking church on a sunny Saturday afternoon on 23 September 1961. We had chosen Old Woking church because it was so beautiful, but in order to be able to marry there we had to deposit a suitcase at our friend Pam's house at Old Woking for a minimum of three weeks before the wedding. Both our families came to Surrey for our big day and the guests were friends from our work places and people we knew socially. My closest friend in Surrey at that time was Don Glazier and I twisted his arm to be my best man. The bridesmaids were my sister Rosie and Joan's sister Christine. The wedding breakfast was held at the local pub. For those that are interested in roses the wedding bouquet was made up of roses I had grown myself and furthermore a variety which I had helped to breed at LeGrice's during my apprenticeship, 'Allgold'. We had a very enjoyable reception and afterwards travelled from Woking to London by train, crossed London by taxi to Liverpool Street Station, and there caught yet another train for our honeymoon destination. I remember looking out of the window to wave goodbye to the guests who had come to see us off and seeing Don, my best man, supervised by the one of the station staff, sweeping up the confetti that had been thrown over us.

For our honeymoon we had hired a boat on the Norfolk Broads, coincidentally named *Happy Days*. Late September/early October is not the best time of the year to be on the Broads. It rained a lot and was very cold. Unfortunately I had forgotten to pack our old Kodak Brownie camera, and with no money to buy another one we arranged by phone for Don to send it on to us care of the post office at Brundall, a village on the River Yare. We boarded *Happy Days* at Beccles, on the River Waveney, so it took us the best part of three days' cruising to get to Brundall, where we discovered that the camera had not yet arrived. Two more days went by before it appeared, which meant that we had only one day left to get the boat back to Beccles in time for handing it in.

Intent on taking as many photos as possible on the last day of our honeymoon, I managed to let go of the steering wheel long enough to run the boat into the reeds near Cantley, on the River Yare. Some passers by in another cruiser offered to help so I threw them a rope to pull us off. However I managed to drop it into the water and it become entangled around the propeller. By now the water in the reeds had become thoroughly churned up and muddy.

There was nothing for it but to strip off to my Y-fronts and dive under the stern to release the rope which, from the constant revving of the engine, was by now truly twisted around the propeller shaft. It took three dives to release it and another one to dislodge the reeds from the propeller. By now several onlookers from other craft had moored on the opposite bank to watch and, when I succeeded and the boat got underway again, I got a rousing round of applause for my efforts. Needless to say I was frozen to the core and it took quite a few tots of whisky to warm me up.

When we arrived back at West Byfleet after the honeymoon, we found a note marked 'Urgent' in the letterbox. It read 'Please telephone me. I would like to see you as soon as possible.' It turned out that the clergyman who married us was in fact a curate and he had got into a muddle with the marriage lines after the ceremony. We had all signed as requested but in effect we were not married at all. Instead Joan's father had married the best man! The incorrect signatures were crossed out and we had to re-sign. The curate then had to initial our signatures, as a witness, to make our marriage legal. He was most embarrassed but we saw the funny side of it.

Just before we were married I managed to scrape together enough money to buy an old 1940 Ford 10 one-ton pick-up truck for just £50. It was in full working order and a lick or two of paint improved its appearance, but I doubt if it would have passed a stringent MOT today. It served us well for almost two years and once I drove it to Pembroke and back to spend Christmas with Joan's parents. It had no heater and the cold draught came in from the ill-fitting doors and windows. We had to scrape the inside of the windscreen constantly in order to see out, and several times we had to stop to scrape the hoar frost from the outside of the windscreen.

We were well wrapped up with windcheaters and gloves but, even so, Joan's feet were frozen. We stopped at Cheltenham, just before the shops closed I recall, and bought her a pair of fur-lined boots, raiding what little Christmas funds we had to do so. This left us with just enough money for the journey and back and a little over to give Joan's parents for our keep. I have vivid memories of that journey. By the time we drove over the Brecon Beacons the full moon was high in the sky and the silhouettes of the mountains stood out dramatically, putting the iciness of the weather into some sort of perspective. Obviously the main consolation was that driving to West Wales in our old banger was far less expensive than travelling there by train.

After living in Mr Orchard's house for about three months we heard of a furnished flat to let, in a large house nearby called Clover Hill. We arranged to go and see it one day after work. The flat turned out to be one large bed-sitting room and it seemed nice and cosy, and big enough for our relatively few requirements. There was a double bed, a Belling cooker and a couple of old-fashioned radiators, which, on that day, were quite warm. There was a small table, with two dining chairs, two easy chairs and a wardrobe. We had to share a bathroom and laundry room with some of the other tenants. We decided to take it. We soon leaned that we had been taken in. On the day we had looked at the 'flat', the landlady had obviously preheated it with loads of electric fires. The radiators did not work too well, so to supplement the heat we had to leave the cooker door open. The cooker, which must have come out of the Ark, took nearly an hour to boil potatoes and sometimes we had to climb into bed fully clothed to keep warm until the dinner was cooked. Occasionally, on very cold nights, we went to bed early to read in order to keep warm and save the cost of the heating.

This particular room had been the dining room of the large house in the days before it was turned into flats. As with most dining rooms in those days, it had a wooden hatch still intact which, although locked, led into the landlady's kitchen. We had not been there very long before her son, who was aged about seven, started to play ball against the hatch. Our requests for him to refrain from doing this were totally ignored.

As newlyweds our time at Clover Hill should have been happy but, to say the least, it was not an easy period. Our old jalopy was not the prettiest of vehicles. There were several other flats at Clover Hill, let to people far more affluent than we were, and their cars were of a far better class. The landlady tactfully asked us if we would mind parking our pick-up truck around the back of the house. She did not need to say why.

Another vivid memory of living at Clover Hill is how I brought rose cuttings home in a briefcase so that I could make them into stocks for budding each evening and plant them the next day at Pirbright. I feel sure that had our landlady known about the cuttings, we would have been asked to leave for lowering the tone of the place. Needless to say we did not stay at Clover Hill for very long, possibly three months.

I heard that a cottage belonging to my boss, Tom Hilling had become vacant. I asked if we could have it and he readily agreed. It was small, with just a kitchen, living room and two bedrooms. There was no bathroom but this was added later. When we moved in it was in a pretty rough state and we redecorated it. Situated in the little hamlet of Pennypot, near Chobham, it had a sizeable garden and was called by the delightful name of 'Myrtle Cottage'. We loved it there. I bought a beehive and a swarm of bees, and started to grow my own vegetables. Before the bathroom was built we were somewhat embarrassed by the antics of the old man who lived in the second of the two cottages. The outdoor toilets of these cottages were built back to back at the end of the gardens and you could be sure that whenever Joan went to use the loo, the old man scurried out to use his. Joan was always aware of his coughing and heavy breathing, not to mention his farting. In the end we decided that he was quite harmless and thought it hilarious.

8

Self-employed in Surrey

Our time at Myrtle Cottage was a happy one but there were, of course, some drawbacks. Although I was close to my work, Joan was seven or so miles from hers at Woking. In the summer she cycled both ways but in the winter I would take her to work early in the mornings in the old Ford truck, with her bicycle on board for her to cycle home in the evenings. The winter of 1963 was particularly harsh. It started to freeze on Boxing Day 1962 and, when the ground was solid, the snow came with a vengeance. The whole of Surrey came to a standstill but, such was the severity of that winter, that no sooner had the roads been cleared the snow came again and again. It did not thaw completely until early March.

When the snow started that Boxing Day, we were visiting Windsor Castle with Joan's parents, Freda and Albert, who had come from Wales to spend Christmas with us. We just made it home in Albert's old Austin Cambridge before we became completely snowed in and were unable to get out for several days. Albert had to return home to Wales to go back to work and therefore had to risk the long journey on treacherous roads. Freda stayed on for a while until we could get her to a railway station.

We were concerned about Albert's journey back because he and his cars were legendary. He always bought them as 'mature' at a time when their owners found them a liability. He was a DIY enthusiast and the first thing he did when he acquired a different car was to go the library and borrow an instruction book for that particular model. When we were riding through Pembroke Dock with him in one of his 'new' cars one day, it suddenly developed a severe wobble and listed to the left. To our utter amazement we watched fascinated as the nearside rear wheel spun past us and came to a stop about a hundred yards ahead. We intended to replace it with the spare but, no surprise, there wasn't one.

By now we had developed a social life – within the limits of our pockets. Our combined pay did not run to much more than a weekly visit to the cinema at Woking and the occasional drink with friends in one of the local pubs. A meal out was a rarity. We also had to keep funds available for visiting our parents once or twice a year.

My hired land was some distance off the beaten track in the middle of Pirbright Woods. The soil was dark and loamy and, in all, the land extended to two acres. A dairy farmer owned it so I had access to plenty of good farmyard muck.

In those days commercial rose production was rather different from what it is today. Rootstocks were produced by making cuttings of a variety of rose called Multiflora de la Grifferaie in the autumn and planting them out in the spring. By the time summer came the resulting plants were budded with named varieties. These days we buy in seedling rose stocks from Holland and plant them, instead of cuttings. I could usually sell all the roses I could produce to the local nurserymen, of whom there were many, within the Woking area. The seedling method of production was just becoming accepted whilst we were living in Myrtle Cottage and, in order to keep as up to date as possible, I ordered and paid for 10,000 of these stocks from Holland. When they arrived I heeled them in at the cottage instead of at the Pirbright field, mainly for my own convenience.

While we were out one day, Tom Hilling paid a surprise visit to Myrtle Cottage. On seeing the stocks, neatly heeled-in in the garden, he must have concluded that I had stolen them from work. A few days later I was summoned to his office and dismissed with no explanation. Despite protestations of innocence on my part, he still would not listen. I was furious that he doubted my word and had difficulty in controlling my temper. My integrity had never been questioned before. I thought afterwards that he probably wanted to get rid of me for financial reasons, as he still would not listen when I tried to show him the receipts for the stocks.

I suspect that Tom's surprise visit was the result of being tipped off by our heavy-breathing old neighbour. Although common practice in the Chobham area, Hilling never really approved of his workers profiting from growing plants on the side – so to speak – even when they had been acquired honestly.

At this point I had worked for Hilling's for about three and a half years and was responsible for the production of 100,000 rose plants annually, mostly Old Garden roses. Working for him was not easy, he was a hard taskmaster. Every few months he was in the habit of turning up at my department in his old prewar grey Bentley saloon and inviting me to ride with him around the entire nursery. One of his pet hates was staff smoking at work. On one of these sorties around the estate, he spotted a woman worker quickly putting out her cigarette when she saw his car but he had already seen the smoke rising through the young trees amongst which she was working. Stopping the car at the end of the row he told me to get out and 'tell that woman that her pocket is on fire'. On another occasion he spotted a vacuum flask standing at the end of one of the rows of young trees. Somehow the car swerved and the flask was squashed!

When Tom Hilling gave me notice he also informed me that he wanted his cottage back within a week, presenting us with quite a quandary. Where could we get accommodation in and around the Woking area in boom times? There were flats available to rent but they were way beyond the means of an out-of-work nurseryman and an industrial nurse. The ignominy of my sudden dismissal was a severe blow to my self-esteem and, for a while, I was extremely depressed and did not know which way to turn. Everything had been going well up until then but because of the irrational behaviour of this arrogant man, it seemed to me that, suddenly, we had no future. We were determined however to vacate the cottage within the stipulated seven days, not only because we felt that I had been badly treated but also because we would not have stayed there any longer even if he had begged us to do so. Of course we could have played dirty and refused to move. He would have had to obtain a court order to get us out. Such action though was alien to our natures. The most positive thing to emerge from this conundrum was the discovery that we had good friends and, as word got out, several of them offered to put us up.

Before we had the chance to accept their generosity we heard of an elderly gentleman who was looking for a couple to share his home in Lightwater, a nearby village. We went to see him straightaway. His name was George Hone and it did not take us long to establish a rapport, agreeing to the arrangement there and then. George was a little nervous of having strangers in his home but went out of his way to please. We reciprocated. In effect we were to have a bedsitting room in his bungalow with the use of kitchen and bathroom.

With our accommodation now assured, I left it until the very last moment of my week's notice, 4.50 pm on the Friday, to return the keys of Myrtle Cottage to Hilling's office. Hilling was there in person and I was able to express my disgust at the way I had been treated with a few well-chosen words. This did no good whatsoever but then I hadn't expected it to. But I felt better. Much better.

As we got to know George Hone, one or both of us would sit with him in the evenings and watch his old black and white television. George, as he insisted we called him, loved documentaries and news programmes. One news item I vividly remember watching in his company was that of the assassination of President Kennedy. George sat there with tears rolling down his cheeks. Most of all, George loved to turn the television off and talk about his exploits as a sergeant in the Royal Flying Corps during the First World War. We loved listening to these stories.

Soon after moving in I noticed a certificate on the wall in the hall signed by Winston Churchill, Secretary of State for War and dated 23 October 1917, stating that George Hone had been mentioned in despatches. When I asked him about this award for bravery he became very reticent but, when pressed, he explained that he had rescued a pilot from a burning aircraft. 'Something anyone would have done,' he said in a dismissive way.

Joan always cooked the evening meal for all of us and, in turn, George prepared lunch for me every day as I had taken to popping home at midday. It was always a plate of beef stew. He made a large amount of this at the beginning of each week in a huge blue enamel saucepan, the stew consisting of a large chunk of stewing beef and as many vegetables as he could get in the pot. This he would reheat every day, first topping it up with water. I wasn't sure just how hygienic this was but it must have been okay because I had no ill effects and it was always very tasty. By the end of the week it was mostly gravy into which he would toss a couple of large, whole onions and a carrot or two.

George was always playing tricks, especially on Joan. One of his favourite pranks was to hang a bell on the springs of one of the two easy chairs in our room. He knew that the first thing she did after cycling home from work was to collapse into a chair. The bell would ring loudly and she would hear George's laughter. He admitted that he did this in order to know when she was home, in case he had dozed off, so that he could make her a cup of tea.

I have already mentioned that I dropped in from work at midday for, by then, I had become self-employed working as a contract worker at various nurseries in the area. I also worked for my friend Don as a bricklayer's labourer. I had received so many offers of work from friends and acquaintances that by now my depression had lifted and I had started to believe in myself again. In the summer I budded roses, for which I was paid by the thousand, a sort of piece-work. This was much more lucrative than working at Hilling's, although being bent double all day it was not easy work. With practice I became very proficient and, on a good day, managed to bud up to 3,000 stocks.

My friend Don, the builder, was blessed with a keen sense of humour. He owned a moped, fashionable in the 1960s, and when he took his driving test, by the time he came to answering the questions at the end of the riding part of the test, he knew he had made too many mistakes to have passed. When the examiner asked 'What is the most important part of your bike, Mr Glazier?' he replied 'The saddle!' 'Why do you say that?' said the examiner. Don retorted 'If you had ridden this bloody moped from Woking to Eastbourne and back as I have, you'd know why.'

On another occasion when we were working for Don, he was seen on a number of days by a security man riding into the building site with what was clearly an empty haversack on his back. At the end of the day this haversack was full up and the same security man's suspicions were aroused. Don was stopped on the way out and asked what was in the haversack. 'Shit' said Don. 'C'mon me lad, less of your lip, I asked you what's in your haversack.' 'Shit' said Don again. Getting rather frustrated, the security man hissed 'I need to look.' 'Okay' said Don, undoing the straps and offering up the haversack. Whereupon the security man stuck his hand into the top of the haversack and brought out a handful of fresh horse manure that Don had been collecting daily for his garden from a bridle path that ran close to the estate on which we were working.

One of the nurseries where I worked budding roses was owned by Alf Small. He was a lovable rogue who never harmed anyone but was an inveterate wheeler and dealer. Although he was a nurseryman he did not grow many plants other than the roses I budded for him. He would take these and other trees and shrubs, purchased from other nurseries, to Covent Garden every week and would return with wads of notes from which he would pay me for my budding in the summer and for the other nursery work I did for him in the winter. It didn't always show with Alf but he would help anyone in need. I came to know him and his family very well.

In the autumn of 1964 we set off to stay with Joan's parents for a week. By then I had been able to buy a much more user-friendly vehicle in the shape of a third or fourth hand Ford Anglia van. I remember clearly that it was a two-tone grey and cream and I felt very important driving it, for the first time, to Wales. By the time we crossed the brand new Severn Bridge into Wales I was feeling decidedly sick with bouts of nasty tummy pains. We stopped for lunch but I could hardly eat. In those pre-motorway days the journey from Woking to Pembroke, even driving the classiest van, took about nine hours.

On arrival I went straight to bed but the pains got worse so I consulted my in-laws' doctor, who thought my problem was caused by something I had eaten, muttering under his breath about transport cafés. He decided I had acid indigestion and gave me a bottle of a horrible-tasting white medicine. After writhing about in bed for two more days Joan asked the doctor to visit me. Within minutes of entering the bedroom he said he would call an ambulance and in less than two hours I was a patient in Withybush Hospital, Haverfordwest. The resident surgeon diagnosed an appendix mass; apparently, had it burst I would have been a goner. I woke up after the operation with tubes coming out of almost every orifice and did not leave the hospital for a further two weeks.

Being self-employed I was not earning anything and, with Joan only having one week's holiday pay, I naturally wanted to get back to Surrey as soon as possible. Against all advice we started back only three days after I was discharged from hospital. How I managed to drive the 300 or so miles back that day I will never know. Joan could only give me moral support, as she had not yet learned to drive. To cap all this, about thirty miles or so from home I had to change a wheel because of a burst tyre.

Two or three days after our return home I was in severe pain again, this time in the pelvic region. My doctor diagnosed a pelvic abscess and because she felt that I had had enough surgery for the time being, she treated me at home with penicillin injections for a few days. Luckily Joan, being a nurse, was able to administer these. After a short period of severe discomfort and high temperatures the abscess came away intact. Within minutes I felt like a new man, the relief was indescribable. That episode behind me I resumed my contract work on various nurseries but it was several weeks before I felt really well again.

It was while working on one of these nurseries that I met Steve Message, who was to become a lifelong friend. I soon discovered that Steve and I had much in common. We were both horticulturists, both ambitious and wanted to become our own boss. We decided to form a partnership and start up a gardening business. We came up with the very original name B & M Gardening Services! With minimal advertising and by word of mouth we found work mowing lawns, cutting hedges and even laying out complete gardens.

As the partnership started to take off we employed a young Italian worker. One of the contracts we secured was the maintenance of the gardens around the hospital at Ascot. Antonio, the Italian worker, was given the job of keeping the lawns cut and tidy. One day, while mowing with a rotary lawn mower in the vicinity of the nurses' swimming pool, he was so intent on eyeing up the nurses he lost concentration and set off in the wrong direction and all the grass cuttings scattered into the pool. It was like a scene from a Laurel and Hardy film – 'What a fine mess you've gotten me into now.' At the time it did not seem funny because, not surprisingly, we lost that particular contract.

B & M Gardening Services occupied all my days but, in the evenings and at weekends, I worked at Pirbright with my roses. In a way though, I always felt that we were building our partnership on straw. Neither of us owned property and unless we could consolidate, we would never succeed in taking the business further.

While we were in Surrey we visited my side of the family far more than Joan's, for the simple reason that Norfolk was much nearer. Nevertheless we tried to visit her family in Wales at least once every year. We usually took our annual holiday in September because it was a quiet time on the nurseries and also because there were fewer holidaymakers milling around the Pembrokeshire countryside at that time of the year. Since she'd lived there all her life Joan knew her way around and we would visit her favourite haunts, including Freshwater West, Broadhaven and St Govan's Chapel near Stack Rocks. Freshwater West has beautiful sands and a rocky shoreline. I, too, had fallen for 'Little England beyond Wales' as this part of Wales is often called. I loved it, especially when the warm west wind was blowing a gale, churning up the angry seas around the rocky coasts. We also loved walking along the cliff tops to the sound of the sea below and the squawks and screeching of the wide variety of sea birds irritated by the human intrusion into their territory.

Pembroke's beautiful castle dates back to Norman times. It was besieged by Oliver Cromwell in the seventeenth century but managed to hold out for a week or so because the Royalists brought food supplies to the castle, in the middle of the night, through a secret passageway that runs under the river from Monkton Priory. This priory is situated on a hill on the opposite bank to the castle. Walking around the castle one day with Joan I spotted a rose flowering amongst scrub and brambles high up on the castle mound. Eager to find out what it was I scrambled my way up through the vegetation to get a closer look. I didn't recognise it immediately but I broke off a piece to take home with me. It turned out to be a plant of one of the first ever Bourbon roses, 'Bourbon Queen', dated 1834. When I told Joan's mother about it she said she remembered seeing this rose growing there when she was a young girl.

At other times during the holiday we would take Joan's family with us to historical places such as St David's Cathedral and Pentre Ifan, a Stone Age burial ground. Sometimes we would drive up into the Prescelly Mountains. Albert loved sea fishing and he and I often fished together at Hobbs Point in Pembroke Dock. Another favourite spot for fishing was from the deck of the first ever iron battleship, the *Warrior*, which, for years, had been moored and allowed to deteriorate in Llanion Cove on the Cleddau river at Pembroke Dock. Some years later, in 1979, this old hulk was towed to Hartlepool where it was restored and made seaworthy again. From there it was taken to Portsmouth and is now a museum.

One day Steve and I spotted an old tumbledown house for sale in the village of West End. The four of us, Steve, his fiancée Barbara, Joan and myself, went to have a look at it and we decided to see if we could borrow enough money to build a pair of semi-detached houses on the site. Neither of us had any idea how to go about raising money but we took advice from Barbara's father and made an appointment with a bank.

The next thing we knew we were sitting in the office of a bank manager in Chobham, nervously putting our ideas to him. I suppose those were the days when bank managers had the discretion to lend money on other criteria than security. To our utter amazement we found ourselves walking out of the bank feeling like millionaires. We had the go ahead to buy the old cottage and land and a promise that, when the plans were drawn up, funds would be available to build our houses.

Barbara had an architect uncle who lived in Devon and our next move was a trip down the A30 to Exeter to give him our brief for a pair of identical three-bedroom, semi-detached chalets. Chalets were the 'in thing' in those days. A week or two later we received the drawings in the post for approval. We all liked the plans and, after getting planning permission from the local authority, the tumbledown house was razed to the ground and the building work started. To save costs we opted to employ craftsmen and workers independently rather than a building firm.

After five or six months Joan and I moved into our very first house, 'Waveney', named after the river on which we had started our honeymoon. Actually to own a house of our own had always seemed an impossible dream, given our backgrounds and upbringing. Until it materialised I had believed that only the very well off could own property. It seemed almost too good to be true. This may sound naïve and it probably was but I had taken the first step in building my future on solid foundations and I started to believe that I could succeed.

It was hard saying goodbye to George Hone but we continued to visit him as often as we could and he came to lunch with us at weekends. As a parting cum house-warming gift, George gave Joan six silver forks and spoons. To me, in spite of my protests, he gave his war medals contained in a brass box from the First World War, identical to those received by all the servicemen for Christmas 1914. The boxes were embossed with the likeness of Queen Mary and originally contained tobacco, I believe. George said he had no one else to give these to, certainly no one who would appreciate their sentimental significance as I would. He also gave me his framed 'Mentioned in Despatches' certificate together with his oak leaf and this is now one of my most treasured possessions. In addition, he gave us one of his souvenirs from the First World War, a small brass candlestick given to him at Ypres by a refugee fleeing from a German-occupied village.

During the time we shared George's home we had grown very attached to him. He was not always in good health but his sense of humour and his mischievous habits belied this fact. We had, in effect, become like a family. He treated me like the son he had never been lucky enough to have. The few years before we met him had been sad and traumatic for him.

When, in the change of life, his wife became mentally ill, his world started to collapse. At first she was admitted to the local mental hospital but it distressed him so much to see her there surrounded by, in his mind, 'crazy people', that he took it upon himself to take her home. He then arranged for different carers to come in and look after her while he was at work. This, however, was doomed to failure because the women he employed did not look after his wife properly and furthermore, he said, various items went 'missing' from the home – china ornaments, silver cutlery, vases etc. Disillusioned and upset he decided that the only thing he could do was to give up work and care for his wife himself.

He had not reached retirement age at this point and giving up his job meant he had to forfeit some of his pension. Gradually his wife's health deteriorated and his savings dwindled away. In order to continue caring for his wife at home George managed to borrow some money from neighbours on the strength of promising them his house after his death. This then was all he had to live on when we first met and I think the rent we paid him helped to keep the wolf from the door.

The mid-1960s were years of plenty, and property values, especially in the Home Counties, were escalating almost daily. This was good for us but B & M Landscapes had difficulty in making enough money to keep both Steve and myself in a lifestyle we would have liked. I so badly wanted to own my own rose nursery but there was little hope of this while we remained in Surrey. Joan was still working but the sizeable mortgage we were paying took a fair chunk out of our joint income. We came to the conclusion that we could not really afford to continue to live at 'Waveney', particularly as we had now been married six years and wanted to start a family. On occasional visits to Norfolk it became clear that the only way forward was to take advantage of the differential values of property between Surrey and Norfolk.

Over two or three weeks we studied all the estate agents' brochures we could get hold of, to find somewhere in Norfolk with land that we could afford. Eventually we found a modest bungalow with two and a half acres in the village of Swardeston, three miles south of Norwich. The price was right so we put 'Waveney' on the market at double the price it had cost to build it and sold it almost immediately. Steve took over B & M Garden Services and we moved to Norfolk. Joan was then three months pregnant with our first child, so it was an opportune time to move. In any case we could never have afforded to continue to live at 'Waveney' without her salary. The move took place in February 1967.

9

Back to My Roots

The deposit for the bungalow and land at Intwood Lane, Swardeston took quite a chunk of the equity released by the sale of 'Waveney' and left precious little capital with which to start to grow roses in Norfolk. I had, of course, left a crop of roses at Pirbright so I hoped to sell these to provide additional income in the coming autumn and winter.

My plan was to start up a new gardening business in Norfolk for the weekdays and work on my newly acquired land in the evenings and at weekends. Our new property included a sizeable old greenhouse and a couple of chicken sheds. That first spring we bought 500 tomato plants for the greenhouse and 100 point of lay chickens for eggs. I also found a bank manager who was prepared to listen to my plans. He gave me a small overdraft on the strength of the crop of roses still growing happily in Surrey, the tomato plants due to come to fruition in June and the chickens who were about to lay. In the event, none of it materialised.

Our new neighbours were an elderly couple who had spent their entire life running a small market garden business growing flowers for cutting, vegetables and tomatoes etc. We came to know Reg and Phyllis Cullum well and they were always very helpful, advising us about tomato culture and egg production. They filled us in with information and gossip about the village and introduced us to the other neighbours in Intwood Lane. There were only half a dozen properties in all. They all took a great interest in what we were doing but they probably thought we were crazy and too ambitious for our own good.

On going back to Surrey to collect my first batch of roses I found that the man I had paid to look after them in my absence had not done his job properly and they had been badly gnawed by rabbits. Almost all of them had been chewed to the point of being unsaleable. When I saw them in this state I was furious with myself because I had not managed to return to inspect them earlier in the summer. I shed a few tears. I had been banking on the proceeds from this crop and, all of a sudden, disaster was staring me in the face once again. What was I going to say to the bank manager, or Joan for that matter? All this on top of the glut in the tomato market (all the growers' tomatoes had ripened at the same time) and when the bottom had fallen out of the egg market too.

Sob stories such as these do not go down well with bank managers, so it was back to see him, cap in hand. We were very lucky to have Mr Offord as our bank manager as he continued to support us, albeit hesitantly. He was so supportive that we referred to him affectionately as 'Daddy Offord'. We became very friendly with him and his wife. They visited us, from time to time, to see the roses in flower. With him monitoring our cash flow and me doing jobbing gardening, we managed to get through the first year and a half, until our first crop of roses grown at Swardeston were ready to be lifted and sold, making us solvent again.

The only thing I took back to Norfolk from Surrey in the end was a black and white Border collie puppy called Twinkle, given to me by the farmer from whom I had rented the land. She was so undernourished that, when Joan saw her, she immediately renamed her 'Twiggy'.

Except for the essentials – curtains, tables, chairs and beds – we had never really furnished 'Waveney' properly with either new or second-hand furniture. We had simply not been able to afford to do so. This meant that we did not have a great deal of stuff to take with us to Swardeston. From time to time, during those first few months, we visited Uncle Ted and Aunt Ethel who lived in the Police House in the village of Foulsham in North Norfolk. Just down the road from where they lived was a second-hand furniture store, more accurately a junk shop owned by a dealer called Philip Phillippo. On these visits we always went to see what bargains he had. We didn't buy rubbish exactly but much of our furniture, at that time, came from him, costing us next to nothing, some of it genuine antiques.

When we first moved to Swardeston Joan experienced some strange vibes whilst redecorating the front bedroom, the one we had

chosen to be the nursery when the time came. I was kept busy outside on the land every hour of daylight and Joan was alone in the
house. She did not know what the problem was but found the
atmosphere in this room somewhat threatening and very oppressive.
She told me about this over supper one evening and I dismissed it as
being the fancies of a pregnant woman coupled with her Celtic psy-
che. Joan was adamant there was something wrong. It was not until
after the baby's birth that the atmosphere lifted. Much later, when
talking to a neighbour, Joan discovered that the last lady of the
house had been taken ill during the menopause and committed sui-
cide by drowning herself in a tin bath near the old greenhouse. Joan
felt that possibly this lady resented her pregnancy, perhaps she had
longed for another child. Who knows?

In spite of being pregnant, Joan did all she could to help keep the
ship afloat, picking tomatoes and collecting eggs were just two of the
jobs she undertook. Our bungalow was of the 1920s ilk, basically a
cube consisting of four main rooms with an added bathroom and
kitchen. It was not in the best of repair. In truth, I was much more
interested in the two and a half acres of land at my disposal to grow
roses than the house and its condition.

Although Joan was three months pregnant when we arrived, not
only did she help on the nursery but she also did most of the interior
decorating. It was while she was standing on a table, painting the
kitchen ceiling, that we first met the vicar of Swardeston. His opening words were 'You silly girl, you shouldn't be painting ceilings in
your condition.' We soon discovered that the Revd Bill Temple-
Bourne was one of the world's eccentrics and totally non-conform-
ist in his approach to his calling. He had been a padre in one of the
Guards Regiments.

It turned out that he was also a rose devotee, so we had much in
common. He visited us regularly and we became very good friends.
We seldom attended his church but he never mentioned this. He
often preached to a very small congregation anyway for his eccen-
tricities, not surprisingly, were misunderstood by the country folk
who were his parishioners. He was also way too outspoken for
them.

Soon after we first met him a notice from the parish council was nailed to the oak tree opposite our gate, inviting all parishioners to attend a meeting in the village hall to discuss urgent matters relating to the church. As a newcomer to the district I felt I should go along to find out what it was about and also to get to know some of the villagers. I was horrified to find that the so-called 'church matters' were in fact a move to defrock the vicar. Apparently this was because he had had the colossal nerve to take it upon himself to give the go ahead for some extra work to be carried out in the church while it was being rewired. Had he not authorised this work while the builders were on site it would still have had to be done later but at double the cost. The extra work amounted to about £500 and the church elders decided that he had gone over their heads in what they termed 'his usual arrogant manner'!

The meeting grew quite heated and everyone there was in favour of getting the vicar moved or defrocked. Witnessing this I felt that had it been a few hundred years earlier, they would have hung him from the nearest tree. With my usual impetuosity I stood up and asked why, in this day and age, the vicar had not been invited to put his side of the story. This was no way for me to make a good impression in the village, rather, to the contrary. I was shouted down. When I left the meeting they were appointing a delegation to visit the bishop to get the vicar removed. They of course failed. A few months later we read in the parish magazine a story written by Bill Bourne. It told the story of country parson who, on his death, had been misdirected to Hell rather than where he naturally expected to go, Heaven. The Devil asked him how he liked being there. The parson replied 'I'd much rather be here than be a vicar in a country parish.'

In September 1967 our first child, Amanda, was born. Like any new father I felt proud and thrilled to bits but at the same time a little daunted by the realisation that I now had extra responsibilities and that a little girl's future wellbeing was basically down to me. A sobering thought. The other aspect was, of course, that I, Peter Beales, was now a father, a father with his own family and the circumstances of my own birth no longer seemed so important. I was a person in my own right. I wanted to do my best for my family and had to balance my ambitions to have my own rose nursery against the security of having a steady income from a nine to five job. Joan and I talked about this and decided that we would move on with our original ambitions. We concluded that, if things didn't work out, the option of getting a job was still there.

Bill Bourne's visits to talk roses every so often came as welcome breaks in my routine, since although I still did part-time gardening I spent a lot of my time working on the nursery. Several of the parishioners, who should have been part of his flock, preferred to attend the church in the next village, called Intwood. One day, while we were talking, he spotted the vicar of Intwood's black Labrador making its way through the roses towards our little dog Twiggy. Bill immediately tried to shoo the Labrador away, saying indignantly 'It's not enough for your master to steal my parishioners, now he's sending you to steal my parishioners' bitches.'

Twiggy had been unwell for some time and was diagnosed as having a urinary infection. Before she could be treated the vet asked us to obtain a sample of her urine. This set us a challenge, how do you collect wee from a bitch? After several attempts, finally resorting to using an old frying pan, I succeeded in getting just enough. Thrilled by my success I ran indoors and telephoned the vet. When my call was answered, I launched straight into a spiel about how clever I had been to collect this sample in this way. The lady to whom I was speaking was quite dismissive and said 'Sorry, you must have the wrong number.'

In December of that year, Amanda, by then known as 'Mandy', was christened in Swardeston church with Bill Bourne officiating. Bill had found a single bloom of 'Zephirine Drouhin' in his garden and placed it on the font for her christening; a lovely thing to do we thought. Twenty-one years later when Mandy got married in November, she carried a bouquet of the same rose. These rose blooms had to be sent to us by airfreight from a rose grower friend in Australia as, obviously, we hadn't any in flower in England at that time of the year.

By now the 20,000 rose stocks, planted earlier in the year, had all been budded and finances became really tight. My bank manager would not give us any more credit and I suppose we were on the edge of bankruptcy, not a nice feeling and I was concerned that I might have to give it all up. One day I heard of a government-sponsored corporation called ACC, Agricultural Credit Corporation. This organisation had been set up to provide guarantees to banks for loans to farmers and growers who were unable to raise capital by any other means. My application was accepted and ten thousand pounds became available to us as working capital. This was a huge relief. We could now move on and I determined to be a little more careful. Ten thousand pounds seemed like a lot of money in 1968 but I was learning the hard way that a lot of money was needed to move the business forward.

Earlier I explained that I had brought our dog Twiggy from Surrey as a puppy. She grew up to be a delight to all the family. She would sit for hours and hours watching over Mandy and, later, Richard when they were babies in their prams, while Joan and I worked on the nursery. If any stranger went anywhere near their prams she would utter a little growl to warn them off. In effect, she was like a nanny to our children. Twiggy also loved playing with shoes and would carry these around the nursery no matter who owned them, never bringing them back to where she had found them. Like most men of the soil I usually took my shoes or boots off on the doorstep and left them there before going indoors and sometimes I would have more than one pair there. Once, when I was late for an appointment to look at a potential customer's garden, in my haste I slipped shoes onto my feet without looking and jumped into my van. I walked around her garden with this lady to see what she wanted done and, just as I was taking my leave, I noticed I was wearing odd shoes, one brown and one black. My potential client could not have failed to notice this herself. I shuffled back to my van feigning a limp but I never did get that job. Who would employ anyone who wore odd shoes and walked with a limp?

For the next year or so I continued coping with the rose crop on my own, with only the occasional help from casual workers. However, when it became time for me to plant my second crop of rose stocks, I had to take on my first employee. Roses take two years to grow into saleable plants, so there are always two crops, a year apart in age, growing side by side at any one time.

By the summer of 1969 my first crop of roses at Swardeston came into flower and I had to think of ways of marketing them. The rose industry had many established names in its ranks and, as a new-comer, it was not easy to become known and accepted. Calling on my experience of exhibiting roses gained as an apprentice at LeGrice's, I put up my first ever exhibit at the Royal Norfolk Show. Of course I had no exhibition equipment such as backcloth, stands and bowls. So, as funds were scarce, I had to improvise. Joan dyed two old bed sheets black for the backcloth. I then made some stands by filling some old-fashioned bakelite lampshades with concrete. The lampshades came from the old chicken shed. While the concrete was still moist a length of 1 in. diameter tubular steel was placed through the hole in the apex of the inverted lampshade. The stands were made in varying heights and pieces of circular plywood were fixed to the tops of the tubular steel rods to support the bowls of roses. For bowls I used 12 in. plastic flowerpots with the drainage holes sealed from the inside with masking tape. Both the bowls and the stands were then painted black.

To carry the roses to the show I begged and borrowed an assort-ment of buckets and containers from my family and the neighbours. We made do with anything that would hold water and was big enough to accommodate about fifty cut blooms. One of the con-tainers was an old lavatory bucket we had found lying around at the nursery. Joan was a little worried that this would be noticed by our fellow exhibitors, one of which was the famous Harry Wheatcroft, so she asked one of our volunteer helpers to be discreet when he car-ried it in to the tent. To our absolute horror, on entering the tent, he called out in a very loud voice with a broad Norfolk accent 'Where d'yer want this here lavatory bucket, Peter?' In fairness, I think he thought it was funny and it did bring smiles to the faces of some of our neighbouring exhibitors.

Our stand consisted of about thirty varieties of modern roses dis-played on a table 20 ft long and 6 ft wide situated on the side of the tent. For this display we were awarded our first ever medal, a silver. This made us feel inordinately proud. We had had a simple little Rose List printed and orders were taken in reasonable numbers. We felt good to have our feet on the first rung of the ladder as recog-nised rose growers. By advertising once a week in our local *Eastern*

Daily Press and by inviting people to visit our modest rose field, we gradually sold more and more roses. That year, at that show, we had our fair share of luck. The show was visited by the Queen Mother and a photograph of her shaking hands with me appeared on the front page of the *Eastern Daily Press*. This bonus publicity worked wonders for us.

In the previous year we had decided to add to our range by growing and selling bedding plants. We sowed seeds of a wide selection of half-hardy annuals such as salvias and petunias. Soon after these had germinated, they all had to be pricked out into special compost, about fifty seedlings per tray. This was very labour intensive and Joan and I worked long into the night filling trays with the seedlings.

That first season we succeeded in filling 2,000 trays and growing them on to saleable size. However, at the peak of the selling season, with only a few days' notice, South Norfolk District Council decided to close our lane in order to install a new water main. No one could get to us by road for about four weeks and all our plans for obtaining full retail prices for our plants were dashed. The only way we could sell them was to take them to local weekly auctions where the prices we obtained barely covered our outlay.

As well as Brian, our one employee, we could always rely on help from my family. I taught my sister Rosie to bud roses and she helped with the budding. My Uncle Walter and a friend of his named Ernie spent a few hours every week at the nursery, for minimum pay, to help with a multiplicity of tasks.

In April 1970 our second child, Richard, was born. I had the son I had always wanted. His birth was very important to me as it meant that my name would be carried over to at least one more generation. He was born at home and although I didn't actually witness the birth, the midwife called me in the minute he was born. I still had to run the nursery and deal with customers while all this was going on. I remember proudly telling our customers that day that I now had a son. One of them gave us a bottle of home-made plum wine that he had found in the boot of his car. We opened it a few evenings later and it was undrinkable, it had gone off – but it's the thought that counts.

Also in that year, by invitation, we exhibited for the first time at

Nanny Beales with Evelyn, Peter's mother, with John and George

Granddad Beales

The author aged two with Peter the dog

The author aged three

Granddad Howes at Buck Brigg

Buck Brigg

LEFT Mum with Walter Howes RIGHT Joan's family. Freda, Albert, Christine and Phillip

Mum, Auntie Ethel and Uncle Ted in the late 1980s

Granddad Howes and Rosie at Buck Brigg

Edward LeGrice

Arthur Clouting and the author with another student receiving their apprenticeship deeds from a representative of the Ministry of Agriculture

Harvesting, 1950s

B Troop, Oswestry, 1956. The author in the bottom left hand corner!

Mine clearing at Trawsfynydd; the author top right

LEFT Farewell to Army friends Les Lee and Derek Isbell at Pembroke Dock
Railway Station RIGHT Graham Stuart Thomas

The author's first vehicle

Rosie, 1960s

The author with the Queen Mother at Sandringham Flower Show, 1969

'Drink a pinta milk a day' 1972

Humphrey Brooke in the early 1980s

Hall Farmhouse, Hargham, 1975

Sandringham Flower Show. Uncle Ted was a police sergeant in West Norfolk and was known to the Show Committee and he put in a good word for us. This show is organised by the Sandringham Estate for the cottagers and the estate workers to show their garden produce. It is an annual one-day event for charity and is always held in late July. The Queen Mother had been a regular visitor to this show for many years as she was always in residence at Sandringham at the time it took place, just before her birthday. Once again Lady Luck was on our side and a photograph was published in the press of the Queen Mother and myself taken at our stand.

At the Norfolk Show in 1971 we introduced our first ever new rose, a salmon-coloured Floribunda seedling that, until a week or so before the show, had not been given a name. At breakfast one day I read in the local newspaper that the latest 'Miss World', Penelope Plummer, was to visit the show. We needed publicity badly at that time and it occurred to me that to name a rose after her might be a good way of achieving it. Although I still blush with embarrassment at the thought (by today's standards not strictly PC), we did achieve coverage with a photograph on the front page of the *Eastern Daily Press*. We also appeared on Anglia Television. This publicity was followed by lots of teasing from my friends but I still have stock of this little rose today, if only for sentimental reasons.

Our business by this time had developed to the point where we did not have enough land to accommodate the additional roses we needed to grow. I managed to rent some from a neighbouring farmer and landowner, Jim Gurney, a member of the famous Gurney banking family. One day I bumped into Jim on my rose field. He was of the opinion that the business would do much better if I had more capital and offered to put in some equity funding. From that point I added a new landscape department to the company. The roses were selling well and there seemed to be a fair amount of landscape gardening work available. We took on extra staff and secured some lucrative contracts.

When Joan and I first started exhibiting roses in London we were aiming for Chelsea but, in order to prove ourselves as it were, we first had to exhibit at several shows in the RHS Halls at Vincent Square, Westminster. Except for size, all the rose growers' stands in those days seemed to be identical, gloriously colourful bowls of roses displayed on tiers, one above the other, boring and almost funereal with little or no individuality. We, however, set out to be innovative by trying all sorts of different approaches. At one show we arranged our bowls of roses on a flat table-like stand in an artistic way and draped the whole with swathes of chiffon. On another occasion we pinned A4-sized cards to the stand, telling the history of each of the varieties on display. Another time we built a pyramid in the centre and placed bowls of roses at differing levels. We tried everything we could to get away from the boringly uniform look. Visitors loved our stands but, alas, the judges were not impressed.

One of the Vincent Square Summer Shows always followed on immediately from the Royal Norfolk Show, in fact the next day. This meant that we had to pull down the stand at Norwich, drive home to Swardeston, load up again with buckets of fresh flowers and drive to London to put the stand up there. It would be late evening by the time we arrived and then we had to build our exhibit, usually finishing this by about two-thirty to three in the morning. One year we actually slept under the stand. We weren't the only exhibitors working there during the wee small hours so we had plenty of company. What didn't help though was the tortuous air conditioner cum heater that hung from the ceiling above our heads. This contraption was on all night. It made a constant whirring and grating noise and believe me, when you are dead tired and struggling to finish your exhibit ready for judging the next morning, this awful noise is enough to drive anyone mad. There was usually a first aid man on duty all night. Joan made use of his services on more than one occasion and had her hot, tired and sometimes swollen feet sprayed with ice-cold foot refresher. Fortunately the show didn't open to the public until 11 am on the first day so we usually managed to get a couple of hours' sleep.

At about this time I applied to the RHS to exhibit at Chelsea Flower Show and, having being vetted, was allocated a 10 ft x 10 ft stand. We were awarded one of the lower grade medals, the Banksian, for this stand. To have been awarded a medal at all was amazing, considering our journey down. We had a Ford Anglia van in those days and the buckets of roses were packed tightly in the back. When we were driving through Whitechapel a pedestrian suddenly stepped out in front of the van and I had to make an emergency stop. Whoosh! All the buckets of roses were thrown all over the place and the water from these filled up the well beneath our seats. It would have been virtually impossible to stop in the middle of London to sort out the mess. I had to drive with about six inches of water around my feet and Joan spent the remainder of the journey with her feet on the dashboard. Our first job after arriving at the show ground was to sort the roses out and refill their buckets. In spite of this misadventure we were lucky because fortune smiled on us again. Ours was only a small stand compared to some others in the marquee but we received more than our fair share of publicity. In those days television cameras needed a mobile generator to supply their electricity. The leads from the generator to the camera were just long enough to reach our stand and no further, so our interview lasted the full three minutes allocated for interviewing all the East Anglian nurseries exhibiting at Chelsea by Anglia Television.

The publicity did us no harm but, in truth, our first Chelsea Show was hardly a raving success in terms of sales. It was a great lesson to us for, on the stand, we had a mixture of both old and modern roses. Almost every order we took was for the Old Garden roses. The competition from all the famous modern rose growers exhibiting there was far too strong for a newcomer like myself to overcome. Nevertheless we had found a niche in the market and, in future years, we showed only Old roses there.

At first we were seen as 'Johnny-come-lateleys' and it took us several years of winning medals and breeding roses before we were welcomed into the ranks. Not only was competition strong but it was very, very difficult to break into the old boy network of the rose trade and, for that matter, the horticultural industry as a whole.

When we first started to exhibit at Chelsea it was in the days of the old marquee that covered an area of three acres, at that time the biggest marquee in the world. It flapped noisily when the wind blew and the light that filtered through the canvas was subdued. The marquee always had a distinctive aroma from the mixture of scents from the varying types of flowers. There was always the sound of water from here and there where fountains were featured in some of the exhibits. Chelsea in those days had a unique almost romantic ambience not totally present in the well-lit spacious new pavilions.

A few years ago they pulled the old marquee down and replaced it, as I mentioned earlier, with bright, full of light pavilions. These are superb but a part of me wishes that some things did not have to change. The old marquee was cut up into suitable lengths and sold on the show ground as souvenirs. I believe that some of the canvas was used by the RHS to make bags and hats. These sold like hot cakes, especially to American and foreign visitors.

To me exhibiting at Chelsea is exciting and rewarding, set as it is in the grounds of the Royal Hospital beside the Chelsea Embankment. The jostling of the crowds visiting the show, the noise, the colour everywhere and the competitiveness of the exhibitors makes Chelsea stand alone amongst gardening shows. Then there are the Chelsea Pensioners who are allowed to wander throughout the show ground at will and are conspicuous in their bright red uniforms. They stop to chat as they pass by from year to year, making friends with the exhibitors and become almost like a Chelsea family.

I started breeding roses seriously soon after arriving at Swardeston, raising over 1,000 seedlings in the first year, amongst them of course 'Penelope Plummer'. Breeding roses is hit and miss. Roses are so highly interbred there can be no certainty what colour offspring may come about from crossing any two varieties, no matter what their colour. At the time of my first venture into hybridising, a red rose held on a strong neck was much sought after. I tried to achieve this by crossing a red rose with a weak neck with a white rose with a strong neck. The result, quite the reverse of my intentions, was another white rose, with a strong neck. It was a good garden rose.

The British Milk Marketing Board were using a catchy slogan in their advertisements 'Drink a pinta milk a day' so I approached them for permission to name my new white rose 'Pinta'. They loved the idea and, after building up a substantial number of plants, we introduced 'Pinta' at Chelsea Flower Show. The well-known celebrity Derek Nimmo came to the show to receive the rose on behalf of the Milk Marketing Board.

Later in the summer we had the rose on show at one of the Royal National Rose Society's shows at the new RHS Hall in London. At this show we were awarded a challenge cup for our display and, when the Milk Marketing Board heard of this, their publicity machine sprang into action. They sent an actor dressed up as a black and white cat to pretend to drink milk from the cup! Joan and I were so embarrassed that we hid behind the stand while all this was going on. All publicity is supposed to be good publicity. What this did to our credibility amongst our peers I dread to think.

A memorable incident concerning the rose 'Pinta' was when Ted Heath, the then Prime Minister, visited our stand. The Milk Marketing Board representative came over to him and told him about their connection to the rose. He looked at Joan and me and laughed uproariously, shaking his shoulders in his customary way. 'Oh, but I never drink milk!' he said.

A month or so after all this publicity I received an order from the City of Columbus, Ohio, USA for several hundred bushes of this rose. Our new customers had seen the name 'Pinta' listed somewhere and had assumed that it had been named for one of Christopher Columbus's ships of that name. They probably still believe this to this day.

Our company now had ten or so employees and was producing 100,000 roses per year. When Richard was about three years old something rather frightening happened. We had called in a local engineer to overhaul our old Ferguson tractor. This he did at the top end of the nursery in an old shed, far away from the house. After he'd gone Richard wandered in to the shed and found a jam jar full of red diesel and petrol mixture used for cleaning the tractor's engine. Attracted by the pretty colour, he drank a little. Fortunately one of our employees, a young lady called Jane, caught him in the act and turned him upside down to make him spit it out. We immediately put him in the car and drove him to the Norfolk and Norwich Hospital Casualty Department. They kept him in overnight for observation as they were afraid the fumes he had inhaled might have damaged his lungs. We learned a valuable lesson to warn our staff and visiting tradesmen not to leave toxic materials within reach of the children.

Jane got on very well with our children and always made time to talk and joke with them. One day when Mandy had wandered up to the packing shed where Jane was working she noticed a large, long handled hook hanging above the door. 'What's that for, Jane?' Mandy wanted to know. 'Oh that's for catching clouds,' Jane replied. The next day, after school, Mandy wandered up to the packing shed again and saw to her amazement a large 'cloud' attached to this hook. Jane said 'It's for you, your very own cloud.' Mandy was thrilled. She was the only little girl she knew of who actually owned a real cloud. Jane had fastened an enormous lump of cotton wool on to the end of the hook. Mandy really believed it was a genuine cloud and kept it in her bedroom for ages

10

Almost Down and Out

Soon after Richard was born and Mandy was about two and a half years old we bought a bungalow at Keswick, about two miles from Swardeston. We did this in order to keep a promise to Uncle Ted. It had always been understood that on his retirement from the Police Force he would join us to become our office manager and live in the nursery bungalow. Our new home was an old lodge and, as well as making improvements, we added two extra rooms. It had belonged to Jim Gurney, by now a fellow director in Peter Beales Roses. We lived there for two very happy years but, by then, our financial state was, once again, becoming quite perilous. The company had developed cash flow problems and I sometimes forfeited my own salary to keep the business going. Joan took a job as a night nurse for three nights a week in a council-run old people's home near Norwich, just to help pay the mortgage and feed us.

The 1970s were difficult years. Inflation was running very high and the rose trade was going through a period of over-production, too many growers chasing too few customers; furthermore, we had supplied lots of roses to garden centres nationally and they, too, were caught up in the same scenario. This meant that it became more and more difficult to get paid on time. One day in August 1974 the crunch came. After consulting our accountant, our bank and the Agricultural Credit Corporation the directors decided that we had no alternative but to call in the Receiver and he put the nursery up for sale. This was one of the worst times of my life, I did not know which way to turn and, to quote Churchill, I had 'a big black dog on my back'. Somehow I pulled myself back from the brink.

I soon realised, after a few hints from the Receiver and from doing a few sums, that if I could raise enough money I could buy the business back. Our Keswick house had appreciated in value considerably in the two years or so that we had lived there and, by selling it and cashing in some endowment policies, I would be able to raise the money I needed. To my horror though, on the day I was due to settle the deal with the Receiver, I was gazumped by a well-known local businessman, who specialised in buying ailing companies.

I had one more card to play. Before all this happened I had been negotiating with Norwich Union Publicity and Marketing Department to name a rose 'Norwich Union' for them. The price had been agreed but the matter had been put on hold while we were financially insecure. I telephoned the Head of Marketing to explain the position, promising him that if Norwich Union would release the funds to buy the rose, I would launch it at Chelsea Flower Show the following spring. They agreed and I felt that the company could soon be mine again, subject to my paying over the money – which I had yet to raise. I must say that the Receiver really wanted me to buy the company back and was very supportive while all the negotiations were going on. In the end I gazumped the gazumper.

We immediately put the Keswick house on the market and a very good friend, Keith Money, of whom more later, told us of a farmhouse to let at Hargham, near Attleborough, belonging to a friend of his. It was in a bad state of repair but the rent asked reflected this, so we accepted. We then had the good fortune to find a cash buyer for our house so, within the stipulated time, the deal was done and the Receiver was able to pay most of the creditors. I had bought my company back.

For a while I used to worry about the morality of what had happened. I eventually came to terms with it in the knowledge that I had paid the price asked and, as well as my company, I was also buying back years of sweat and tears. I was now thirty-nine years old and, to use an old cliché, I had been 'through the University of Life', from being a country bumpkin to experiencing all the ups and downs in the passage of time. All this had given me more confidence and I was now better equipped to deal with most situations. One of the most important things I learned was how to hold a conversation with anyone I rubbed shoulders with, at any level of society.

There were lots of advantages to what I had done. I still had all our stock of roses and I was able to close down the unprofitable landscape department. I kept Uncle Ted on to run the office. One of the conditions attached to my buyback of the business was vacant possession of the bungalow and Ted and Ethel were in the process of looking for another house. I was, however, able to keep the land until the roses were mature. I also took on a young school leaver named Ian Limmer as an apprentice. Ian is now our Nursery Manager and a vital part of our business. His mother had previously worked for us in our office and I re-employed her as a part-time secretary. The only other person I kept on from the old company was a man named Eddie Sparks, who was getting on a bit but was a very experienced rose grower.

While having lunch at the White Lodge pub in Attleborough one day, I met a local farmer and we got talking. When the conversation got round to the availability of land in the Attleborough area, he told me that the field of eleven acres adjacent to the pub, running alongside the London to Norwich trunk road, was up for sale. So it was once again cap in hand to our bank manager. The next day I made an offer for the land. After a bit of wrangling with the elderly farmer who owned it, we arrived at what seemed to me a fair price. This was one of the first significant things I did after getting my business back but there were many more still to come in the coming decade.

Within days of moving in to Hall Farm House we started renovating and decorating. All the family helped, especially Ethel and my mother who by now had been a widow for about seven years. It was a labour of love. I left them to it to go backwards and forwards to Swardeston, a forty-mile journey every day. The farmhouse had been built in Victorian times, as an addition to a much older seventeenth-century house. It had not been occupied for at least ten years and probably not decorated for twenty years before that. Old newspapers discovered beneath the rotting linoleum on the floors were dated 1947. We learned that it had been commandeered as officers' quarters throughout the war and there was plenty of evidence of army occupation, especially in the outhouses, which had clearly been built by the military. Indeed one was an old Nissen hut.

After working at Swardeston all day I seldom arrived back home until late in the evening, usually to find yet another part of one of the ten rooms had been decorated. The children were still attending school at Cringleford and it was quite a journey for Joan and them every day. Ted and Ethel had now found somewhere else to live so we decided to move back to the bungalow at Swardeston for a short period, until the nursery at Attleborough was up and running. As we still had stock there the Receiver allowed us to rent the bungalow for this interim period.

The bungalow and nursery at Swardeston were situated halfway up a fairly steep hill. During that winter snow came with a vengeance. This was exciting for the children – they loved sliding and tobogganing down the hill – but we were literally snowed in. It was the worst winter we had experienced since moving from Surrey. Intwood Lane, being a minor road, was one of the last to be cleared which meant that we were cut off for a couple of weeks and the children could not go to school.

The nearest shop was about a mile away down the hill in the centre of Swardeston, with the bigger supermarket-type shop about two miles in the opposite direction in the village of Eaton, near Cringleford, and uphill most of the way. On the first day of the heavy snowstorm, together with our neighbours, we cleared the snow from around each property as best we could. We needed to get to the nearest shop as supplies were getting low; this meant shanks's pony. In particular we needed medical supplies as we had all caught colds. Warmly wrapped up we set off across the fields because the lane was packed high with snow blown into it by the strong north-easterly wind. It was tough going but we made it back home at dusk, exhausted and footsore but with enough food and medicine to last a while.

After two weeks or so the children were able to return to school. However the snow was still lying around here and there and Richard and his school friends played snowballs at every opportunity. At playtime one day the boys decided it would be good fun to snowball the headmaster's car. Richard must have unknowingly rolled a stone into one of his snowballs, or so he said. He aimed it at the car and was horrified to see that it had cracked the windscreen. The teachers were in the staff room having their break and were rather surprised when a knock came on the door. The headmaster opened the door and Richard, in a small voice, said, 'Please sir, I've broken your car window.' Mr Leamon was so taken aback that Richard had voluntarily owned up that he never punished him.

It was at this time that I went down with pneumonia, an experience I never want to repeat. After a couple of weeks on antibiotics and being looked after by Joan I was up and about again, but it was several more weeks before I was completely recovered. This illness left me with the lower half of my left lung badly scarred, which has caused me respiratory problems ever since.

In May 1978 Joan's mother sadly passed away. She had been ill for several months and it was all very traumatic. Joan travelled by coach to Wales most weekends towards the end. When Freda was first taken ill no one seemed to know what was wrong. Eventually she was diagnosed as having an inoperable brain tumour. Mandy and Richard were very upset at losing their granny, especially Mandy who had always been very close to her.

A year later, when the nursery move was complete, we returned to Hall Farmhouse permanently. We decided that the exterior of the house needed decorating and we found part-time help from an elderly, character called Jim Skipper who had just moved to Norfolk from Essex. Jim loved working for us and we became very fond of him. He continued to work for us until he was well into his eighties. He had been a soldier and had fought with the Desert Rats and in Italy. He liked nothing more than telling our staff and us about his army exploits. During the time Jim worked for us he became very attached to the nursery and loved working in the rose gardens. He once told me that if he were to die suddenly he would like it to be amongst the roses and his friends, our staff.

Moving a rose nursery is fraught with problems, because it takes two years to produce a rosebush. This meant that for the first year after our move to Attleborough there was a crop growing in two different places, twenty miles apart. We also needed an office in both places so, following the planting of the rose stocks at Attleborough, I purchased a large second-hand caravan and placed it in the corner of the field. Initially this served as a mess room for the staff, a storeroom for tools and somewhere to accommodate the office and nursery equipment as and when it was brought from Swardeston. Suffice to say that over the next few months the move was completed and we were ensconced at Attleborough, where we remain to this day.

New Roses, New Books and New Friends

The first rose I introduced after moving to Attleborough was called 'Norwich Castle'. It is still one of our best-selling Floribundas. Its colour is very like that of bitter ale. In fact it was sponsored by the then Norwich Brewery, who really wanted to call it 'Norwich Bitter' after one of their beers. When I objected, the managing director of the brewery agreed that such a name would never sell a rose. Thankfully, it became, as I had planned, 'Norwich Castle' which in fact was the Brewery's logo.

I cannot remember when it was that I first met Keith Money but he came to the nursery one day, while we were still at Swardeston, to take a look at my rose collection. He was clearly passionate about roses and convinced me that I should go and have a look at his rose garden and perhaps identify those he had been unable to name. A few days later I spent a whole day with him, just looking at roses and partaking of numerous glasses of wine. I was staggered by the extent of his collection and fascinated by the rarity of some of them. He had rediscovered some of the roses when visiting other gardens or had simply purloined them from the gardens of empty or derelict houses. From that day on we have been firm friends.

Throughout the 1970s and early 1980s, finding the funds to print a colour catalogue was always a problem and one day I had the idea of getting it done at someone else's expense by having it published as a booklet. It was a long shot but I approached Jarrolds, a well-known Norfolk publisher of educational books. One of Keith's several talents was photography and, in all honesty, although I wrote the text it was Keith's pictures that appealed most to Jarrolds from a marketing point of view. It transpired that our little booklets, originally meant as catalogues of roses, found their way all over the world and were responsible for bringing my name to a much wider audience than I had ever thought possible. The booklets – there were four of them – were based entirely on the history of roses and their development over the years. The first two published were *Georgian and Regency Roses* and *Early Victorian Roses*, followed quickly by *Late Victorian Roses* and *Edwardian Roses*.

I have already mentioned Keith's photography; he is also a gifted watercolour artist and an eminent author specialising in the ballet. Amongst his published works are biographies of Anna Pavlova and Margot Fonteyn. It was at the time of the publication of Pavlova's life story that Keith asked me if one of my roses could be named 'Anna Pavlova' to celebrate the launch of his book. I gave him the freedom of the batch of my unnamed seedlings from which to make his choice. He selected one that I thought not floriferous enough. It has a very strong fragrance and is a beautiful soft pink colour. I hesitantly went along with his choice, thinking it would end up an also ran. 'Anna Pavlova' remains one of our best-selling roses to this day. This goes to show that I am not as good a rose judge as I had thought and, to rub it in, the rose was awarded a silver medal at the Genoa Rose Trials for, would you believe, freedom of flower!

On Christmas Eve 1981 we received a telephone call from Joan's cousin in Wales. She rang to tell us that Joan's dad Albert had died suddenly. Naturally Joan was very upset and we made plans to travel back to Wales. We decided to let the children enjoy their Christmas Day before we explained to them that their granddad had died and then drive to Wales on Boxing Day. It appeared that Albert had had a blood clot in the aorta and his death had been instantaneous. It was just over two and a half years since Freda had died and although Albert came to Norfolk to stay with us during that time, and we went to Wales to see him, he was very lonely without her. As with their granny's death, Mandy and Richard were very upset. They had lost both their Welsh grandparents now. Richard was inconsolable at first because he idolised his granddad.

As time went on during those early years of the 1980s, our efforts to establish ourselves at Attleborough were paying off. We began to gain a reputation for the quality of our roses and our service. Our catalogue too, although still a modest publication compared to those of our competitors, was becoming known for having the most comprehensive list of Shrub and Old Garden roses in the UK. The fact that we were now situated beside a main trunk road was a big advantage. Shows were also becoming important to us, not only from the point of view of sales but as vehicles for free publicity, as more and more garden writers realised that we were offering something 'different' to the rose-growing world.

There was a pleasing hint that we were becoming known for our rose collection when one day I received a letter from Australia, addressed to 'The Old Rose Grower, England'. Another letter I still have in my memorabilia came from Ireland. The envelope had clearly been nibbled and there was a note on the corner of it, presumably from the postman who collected it, apologising for 'the snails in the letterbox'.

A delightful, elderly eccentric I came to know well in the early 1980 was Humphrey Brooke from Claydon in Suffolk. He had amassed a sizeable collection of old roses in his large, informal, inimitable garden at Lime Kiln. There had once been a lime pit there so it is not surprising that his roses struggled. The well-being of his roses did not concern Humphrey; he only saw in them what he wanted to see. His garden was open to the public and he had no hesitation in ordering anyone who dared to criticise his roses out of his garden, making it very clear with a few well-chosen Anglo-Saxon words that they were never to return. Humphrey gave me several of the roses that I have in my own collection to this day; one is particular is 'Sophie's Perpetual'.

When I first met him, Humphrey was already retired, having worked for several years as Secretary to the Royal Academy. For various reasons, not of my concern, I believe he left the RA under a cloud, thus exacerbating the bouts of depression from which he had always suffered. All roses had to be old and of quiet colours for Humphrey. I recall a visit he made to the nursery at the time when the coal miners' strike was at its height. On arrival, he noticed a tall plant of 'Alexander', a bright vermilion rose. 'What are you doing growing that Arthur Scargill type rose?' he exclaimed.

As the 1980s progressed, what was initially a rose field at

Attleborough began to look like a nursery. We added an extra por-
tacabin as a sales point, together with a toilet block and a hard-
standing area for parking. After several attempts we eventually
obtained planning permission to put up a name board. We also
bought two 50 ft polythene tunnels and a second-hand greenhouse.
The latter enabled me to continue with my hybridising.

In 1981 we employed Simon White, who is still with us today and
is now our Customer Services Manager. When I first interviewed him
he was still at school and seemed too frail physically ever to become
a nurseryman. But he put on weight and I was soon proved wrong.
He is now a valuable member of our team and, like our Manager
Ian, is recognised throughout the country as an authority on roses.
He occasionally lectures to horticultural societies throughout East
Anglia.

Before we left Swardeston our friend the Revd Bill Bourne had
retired and had moved to Wymondham where he planted a small
rose garden. Amongst his roses was a lovely, fragrant, red rose called
'Alec's Red'. His excitement knew no bounds when this rose sported
and he came to see me at Attleborough carrying a beautiful pink
bloom. We propagated this rose for him and when it continued to
come true we introduced it for him as 'Uncle Bill', the name by
which our children had always called him.

During the trial period for his rose Bill often came to the nursery
and on one of these visits he turned up with a large dressing on his
head and a swollen, black and blue nose. 'What on earth have you
been up to, Bill?' I said. Bill had a Doberman pinscher. He had been
taking it for a walk, on a lead, when it caught sight of a cat on the
other side of the road. He couldn't hold it back, was towed along,
and cannoned into a lamp post. 'The next thing I knew was when I
came to with a throbbing head and no dog. My next dog will be a
Yorkie!'

Another interesting person I came to know at about this time was
Christopher Lloyd, the owner of Great Dixter in Sussex. I can usually rub along with anyone whatever his or her point of view but I
cannot bear rudeness or pomposity and Lloyd had more than his fair
share of both. I had no problem with his writing style which was
always scholarly. He had built up a big following and one day he

announced to the world that he was thoroughly fed up with his roses and that he had dug them all up and replaced them with brightly coloured plants such as cannas. Furthermore he suggested that everyone else should do likewise because roses are hard work, disease-ridden and need pruning every year. I happened to know that most of his roses were very brightly-coloured modern Hybrid Teas and the like, which are the most difficult to grow anyway. The rose fraternity was incensed by what he had written and I took it upon myself to write to him in an effort to open a dialogue with him about roses to advise him that many of the Old Garden and shrub roses are much easier to grow, adding that I would be very happy to send him some complimentary plants for him to try. After some time I received a very rude reply, effectively saying that I should mind my own business and suggesting that rose growers would be better off growing bedding plants.

I decided there was not much I could do to change his mind and left it at that. Nevertheless it left a sour taste, as I don't like bearing grudges. For years afterwards I watched Lloyd as he wandered past our stand at Chelsea, totally ignoring our exhibit and me in particular. When I became President of the National Rose Society I received a hand-written card from him wishing me good luck, an olive branch which I readily took. When I heard recently that he had passed away I must admit that I felt relieved that we had patched up our differences while he was still alive and well.

The early 1980s became a time of plenty for us. We were making our presence felt at shows around the country. I always helped to put up the stands but I only took part in selling the roses reluctantly, finding it increasingly difficult not to show my boredom at having to answer so many of the same questions over and over again. In fact, both my staff and Joan would do their best to keep me away from customers, their actions justified when Joan overheard a lady saying 'There, I told you, he looks exactly like Heathcliff!'

Up until now ours had been the only nursery showing Old Fashioned roses at Chelsea and we had built up quite a significant clientele of devotees for this type of rose. We knew that inevitably the increasing popularity of these roses would bring other growers into the market and we had become aware of several of these emerging in various parts of the country, the best known of which was David Austin of Albrighton, Staffordshire. In 1982 he started showing at Chelsea and this was the beginning of friendly one-upmanship between our two companies. One of the nice things about the horticultural industry is the respect we have for one another and even though we competed against each other for the medals we always enjoyed doing so. In fact it kept both companies on their toes. Over the years we have competed with each other I have come to look upon this quiet-spoken, self-effacing gentleman as a friend. He and I often get together at Chelsea for a good old chinwag and compare notes about the state of the rose market. David has taken our shared love for the Old Fashioned varieties several steps further than I have and introduced, over the years, a range of what might loosely be called reproduction roses; in other words bringing the form and fragrance of the old varieties into his own range of shrub roses which he has called 'New English Roses'. David knows, I think, that I disagree with his choice of name for this strain. If these roses are new English roses then so are mine and, likewise, those of all the other English rose breeders. I believe their collective name should, more correctly, be 'Austin's Roses'. I do not intend these comments to take anything away from his achievement in producing a group of varieties that have already made a significant contribution to today's world of roses.

We were now going as far afield as Edinburgh and Cornwall to exhibit at shows. This was very demanding on our staff and, in order for Joan to be able to go, we used to take Mandy and Richard to stay with my mother and Rosie, at least during the school holidays. Chelsea Flower Show always came in term time in May each year so Mum would come and stay with the children at our house. At some of the other shows Joan and our then office manager, Heather, would look after the stands on their own, releasing the nursery staff for other essential work.

As we became better known customers brought or sent roses to me for identification. Some were just commonplace, others I had not come across before and, now and again, a rare variety. I encouraged this because in addition to supplying a service, it meant that I was able to add to my own collection. When the rose needing identifying turned out to be rare the customer was thrilled to know its name and only too pleased to know that we would conserve it and offer it in our catalogue.

A customer turned up one day with a whole basket of roses to be identified. Although she insisted that she had an appointment there was nothing in my diary to say she was coming. I was actually at home getting ready to go to Yorkshire on business and already running late when the office telephoned me to say that this lady demanded my personal attention. I didn't want to offend her so went back, albeit reluctantly, to the nursery. Whilst waiting for me to come, she had neatly laid out her specimens on a table in our greenhouse. She went on at some length about my failure to keep her supposed appointment, saying she had travelled such a long way – in fact from Cambridge.

As I always do, I examined each one of the roses carefully, working systematically through the pile. I recognised them all and, picking them up one by one, I told her their names. Early on in this sequence she started to challenge me, saying things like 'It can't possibly be that because my friend has one of those and it's totally different.' With one eye on the clock because I was by now running quite late, I tried hard to keep my cool. However, after she contradicted me a few more times, I swept all her roses off the table with one sweep of my hand and jumped up and down on them until they resembled a mess of potpourri. 'Madam,' I said, 'if you already knew the names of these roses, why did you come and waste my time? Goodbye.' I don't feel particularly proud about the way I behaved on that occasion but there we are.

'The customer is always right' is not an assumption that I can easily swallow; it's also true to say that 'you can't please all the people all the time'. Like all businesses serving the general public we occasionally come across a decidedly difficult customer. One day I received a letter of complaint from a lady who thought her rose had too many thorns. She went into great detail about how her grandchildren had scratched themselves, then, to my delight, ended her letter with 'I am not buying any more of your roses' and signed it 'An unsatisfactory customer'.

After we had been at Hall Farm House for about three years our faithful Border collie Twiggy died and there were tears all round. She had been such a faithful pet and very devoted to Mandy and Richard who were now aged fourteen and eleven respectively. Already Mandy was making herself useful on the nursery at weekends, watering and weeding.

Winning gold medals at all the provincial shows was becoming a regular occurrence but the one we wanted most, a 'Gold' at Chelsea, somehow eluded us. It was not that we didn't try but Old Garden roses are amongst the most difficult of flowering shrubs to exhibit. We had to produce about twice as many plants as were needed, selecting only the best for the show. Although we continued to enlarge the size of our stand each year, the judges still did not seem to consider it worth a 'Gold'. Most years we narrowly missed out and had to be content with lower grade medals. Neither our customers nor staff could understand their ruling.

Judging at Chelsea Flower Show is a huge job. How can you compare a geranium to a rose? The RHS makes up its judging panels in teams of twelve and there are usually four such panels judging all the exhibits. The awards are based on a show of hands from each member of the team according to the recommendation of their chairman. If, for example, he thinks a stand is worth a silver medal that is what it will get if the majority agree. The trouble is that these panels of judges are made up of some amateur gardeners and some professionals who may or may not know much about the genus they are expected to judge. I was always perturbed by the fact that for several years one or two professional rose growers, themselves exhibiting at Chelsea, were part of the panel of judges for our stand. This cannot be right.

Having been in place since Chelsea Flower Show was inaugurated in 1913, the judging system has now become outdated. I believe the RHS think they are being fair but for a number of years I have thought that the judging system would be improved if each panel consisted of only three judges, each a specialist in the particular genera they are asked to judge. I also believe that these three judges should be recruited from overseas so that they can be completely objective.

Over the years I have challenged the judges' decision on more than one occasion but it's like knocking your head against a brick wall. After such a challenge the chairman of the judging panel will sometimes come to take another look at the stand, ostensibly to re-evaluate it but I have never known it to make any difference. I believe that more exhibitors would complain at the quality of judging if they didn't feel that by doing so they would not be invited to exhibit there again.

I had met Clarissa Mason, wife of the famous actor James Mason, at a rose show and we got chatting. Clarissa loved roses and knew a great deal about them. She had already had a rose named for her by another grower but James had not. After our little chat she took home some photographs of one of my seedlings for James to see. The rose is a very dark red semi-double hybrid Gallica with a lovely boss of golden stamens. It seemed right for James's personality. After its introduction at Chelsea Flower Show attended by the Masons, I sent some bushes to their home in Switzerland. When they flowered the following summer, James was thrilled with 'his rose' and telephoned us to say how very much he loved it. Sadly, a month or so later, he died. He was a very out of the ordinary actor and his rose has the same quality.

Another rose we introduced at Chelsea was for the Sadler's Wells Ballet Company's Tercentenary. This rose is still very popular, especially as a hedging variety. Its colour is cherry-red and silver. We liked the name 'Sadler's Wells' and it generated some good publicity for us.

The Ballet Company had arranged for Lesley Collier, the prima ballerina, to visit our stand at Chelsea to be given a bouquet of the rose at its launch on Press Day. It had been agreed that I should meet her on the Chelsea Embankment, outside the main gate of the show, to escort her to the stand and in order for us to be able to recognise each other we each had to wear a rose. I arrived at the prearranged meeting place in good time but there were already crowds of people there. Then came an announcement over the public address system: 'Would all exhibitors and visitors kindly leave the showground in an orderly fashion immediately.' It was a bomb scare.

Later, I learned that the IRA had informed the police that a bomb had been concealed somewhere among the exhibits. The already crowded pavements on the Chelsea Embankment were besieged with agitated people, lots of them wearing roses as buttonholes. Eventually, after about an hour, the 'all clear' came and we were allowed back in. It had turned out to be a hoax. I made my way back through the melee to the stand, praying that I had not missed Miss Collier. I was met by an irate reporter who wanted to know where I had been. Apparently the ballerina had been one of the first to gain entrance to the showground when the 'all clear' sounded. She had received her bouquet from a member of staff who had also managed to get back to the stand on time, posed for the camera holding the bouquet of 'Sadler's Wells' roses and, her work finished, had wandered off to look around the rest of the show. Sadly, I never did have the privilege of meeting her but at least the rose was launched.

It was now two years since Twiggy had died and the whole family missed having a dog about the place. We decided it was time to get another one, preferably another Border collie, so we kept our eyes on the 'dogs for sale' column in our local newspaper. It was not long before an advert appeared that sounded promising.

A few days later we all travelled to March in Cambridgeshire to look at a litter of puppies ready to leave their mother. There were six left out of a litter of eight. One of them was black, white and tan with a distinctive black heart-shaped patch on its side. This puppy made a big fuss of the children and we fell in love with it. On the way home we named it 'Patchy'. Patchy's parents were both champions in the Welsh Sheep Dog Trials but although we were suitably impressed we just needed a loving pet and this is what she soon became. When she had to be put to sleep in autumn 1994, it was so distressing that Joan vowed never to have another dog (although she subsequently did).

1985 was the seventieth anniversary of the execution of Edith Cavell. (Incidentally the First World War heroine was born in the vicarage at Swardeston where her father was vicar.) The Revd Philip McFadden, who had taken over from Bill Bourne as vicar at Swardeston, decided he would like to mark the anniversary by having some bushes of 'Edith Cavell' roses planted around her memorial in the village. He approached me to ask if we could supply the roses but an extensive search via the Royal National Rose Society drew a blank. It seemed that this rose was now commercially extinct. However, given that it was introduced in 1919 by Henry Morse and Sons, a famous Norfolk rose nursery, it seemed likely that someone in Norfolk still had plants of this variety.

I wrote to the *Eastern Daily Press* asking if anyone had an 'Edith Cavell' rose. I received about half a dozen replies but, although I followed them all up, none of them were the correct variety. A little while later I received a letter from a lady in Brundall, a village near the Broads, telling me that her neighbour had this rose in her garden and could prove its authenticity. I contacted her and she made arrangements for me to meet her neighbour, a Mrs Doris Devine. The first thing I noticed as I entered her garden was a somewhat impoverished rose bush bearing one little cluster of red flowers. I knew that, at last, I had found the rose I was looking for. Over a cup of tea Mrs Devine showed me a card on which was written 'To George and Doris on your first wedding anniversary, six plants of Edith Cavell'.

George and Doris were married in 1934 and although they had moved house a few times while George was still alive, they had always taken their rose bushes with them. The plant I saw was the only one left and she gave me permission to take a few budding eyes for propagation. In due course I was able to provide the Revd Philip Mcfadden with the roses. To bring this story up to date, I recently saw them growing happily below Nurse Edith Cavell's memorial; yet another rose had been saved from extinction. Many years later, in 2003, we supplied some more plants of this rose to the City of Norwich and Joan and I attended the ceremonial planting below Edith Cavell's statue just outside the Erpingham Gate of Norwich Cathedral. The Bishop of Norwich blessed the roses and every time I drive through the city I glance over to see how they are getting on.

I was busy budding roses on a cloudy Sunday afternoon in October 1983 when, just as I was about to finish for the day, a visitor came to the nursery, holding one of my little Jarrolds booklets in his hand. He introduced himself as Christopher MacLehose of the Harvill Press. Waving the little book, his opening words were, 'Would you like to write a book on roses for publication in time for

Christmas 1985?' He went on to say that he liked what I had written in the four Jarrolds booklets and that he would like the book to be on old-fashioned shrub roses, climbers and ramblers and that I would have complete freedom to tackle the subject in any way I wished. He said he had just been to Norwich and had no more time to go into details since he had to be in London that evening. He added that he would telephone me the next day.

By the time I arrived home to tell the family, I was very excited. I spent most of that night unable to sleep, lying in bed planning how I would tackle the book and speculating on how it would look. It had always been a secret ambition of mine to write a proper book. It was just about lunchtime the next day when Christopher telephoned as promised and, after what seemed a very short conversation for something so important, we had agreed the advance I would receive, the royalties I would get and the date for the delivery of the finished manuscript.

Two days later the contract arrived by post for signing together with a cheque as an advance. It was not until I actually had the contract in my hand that I really believed it was happening. It took well over a year to complete the book that, after much thought, was entitled *Classic Roses*. I wrote every word by hand, with Joan doing all the typing. These were the days before word processors and she used an old-fashioned Imperial typewriter. In the end she must have typed the whole book at least five or six times. After each section had been typed I would edit, correct and change my work over and over again to get it to my satisfaction. (I still write everything by hand today, but with more confidence; so there are not so many corrections. In any case it is easier to make changes on screen with a computer.)

I wrote *Classic Roses* in our dining room which at that time served as an office and a library, for by then I had amassed a sizeable collection of books. Joan sat at the deal-topped table in the draughty, old-fashioned, quarry-tiled kitchen to do the typing. I used two exercise books, alternately writing in one while Joan typed as far as she could from the other. Then we would change over, and so on.

In the late 1970s I had taught myself photography, having acquired a second-hand 35 mm Pentax SLR camera from an auction, so my slide collection was by this time fairly extensive. Even so

I needed many more pictures for the book than I could provide, so I begged and borrowed from various rose friends. One, in particular, was Dick Balfour, a past President of the Royal National Rose Society, and, another, Vincent Page, a rose devotee who, at that time, was the picture editor for the *Sunday Times Magazine*. I was also fortunate to have a rose lover as my designer. Vera Brice worked for the Harvill Press and she and I formed a good partnership. *Classic Roses* came out in time for Christmas 1985 and was published simultaneously in America.

The title of the book came about during dinner in Keith Money's farmhouse at Caston. We had been exchanging ideas for the title throughout the meal but most of the more obvious titles had already been used. It was over coffee that I finally decided on *Classic Roses*. As the book became more widely read and recognised as a significant addition to rose literature, I began to realise that the term 'Classic Roses' was becoming accepted as a generic term for roses of the type discussed and described in my book. So much so that it became necessary to define the term in broad understandable parlance. I believe a classic rose to be a shrub rose of any type that fits into the landscape it serves without screaming back at us. For example, if it is of a quiet pastel shade it should be planted in schemes of a soft colour but if is a brighter, more cheerful rose it can be used amongst the louder, noisier colours. The roses excluded from this definition are the modern Hybrid Teas and Floribundas which are usually relatively short growing with an upright habit and used for massed planting and are difficult mixers except with their own kind.

Within weeks of hitting the bookshops it became clear that its timing was good. Since Graham Stuart Thomas's books in the 1960s, no one had written a book devoted to old roses; at least not one as comprehensive as mine. It received good reviews worldwide and soon a reprint was necessary to meet demand. I will never forget the thrill of actually holding my book for the first time that day in November 1985. When I think back, it now seems silly how self-satisfied I felt seeing my name on the spine of a book, which had anyway been a labour of love. Nor, at that time, could I even begin to guess just what a difference it was going to make to my life.

When I was about halfway through writing the book it became

obvious that working on it in my spare time only was not enough. I needed to spend as much time as possible writing, so I left the nursery under the control of my then Manager who had not been with us long. On my return to work I soon discovered that my staff had become very unsettled under his irresponsible leadership. There were many fences to mend, with both staff and customers. I encouraged him to leave and appointed Ian Limmer in his place. Although still relatively young Ian knew his job and had the respect of his colleagues. His loyalty to the company is beyond doubt. I have never had cause to regret my decision. Nowadays Ian's skill and knowledge of roses is recognised throughout the rose world and he, Mandy and Richard all work well together as a team. Ian's rose devotee wife Tina is also a valuable member of our customer relations team.

12

Rossini, Thunderstorms and Down Under

As *Classic Roses* became widely distributed, invitations to lecture started to come in from all corners of the world. I had been lecturing to local East Anglian horticultural societies for some time, focusing mainly on Old roses. The first invitation to speak overseas came from the World Federation of Rose Societies, asking me to lecture at their Convention in Toronto. Unfortunately I caught 'flu just before I was due to fly so had to cancel. This was a great disappointment to me because it would have been my first ever long-haul flight. I didn't like letting them down at the last minute but was able, a few years later, to visit Toronto and put things right.

One day I received a telephone call from Marjorie Barton of Sunderland. She asked for my help. She needed about 1,000 blooms of Old roses for a Festival of Rossini Music and Song to be held in Bishopwearmouth church the following week. I can't think why I agreed to this because the logistics were clearly going to be difficult. Marj was very persuasive, however, and I found myself, very early one morning, setting off north with a vanload of roses. Because of the heavy traffic en route I was somewhat late arriving and all the Geordie ladies of the flower club were on tenterhooks, as they now had only a limited time in which to arrange the roses in the church. They were so relieved that I had finally turned up that they smothered me with hugs and kisses. In spite of their belated start, these ladies produced some fantastic arrangements and I was told later that when the soprano hit top C lots of the petals from my roses fluttered to the floor.

Earlier that same year I flew with Joan and Richard to Jersey for a short holiday. Whilst walking in one of the island's narrow lanes, I spotted a rose I did not recognise growing near the garden gate of a cottage. It excited my curiosity so much that I knocked on the front door with the intention of asking the owner if he or she knew what the rose was called. My luck was out, there was no one at home, so, disappointed, I turned to leave. However, it so happened that on my way back to the garden gate a shoot of this rose somehow caught on my trouser leg and I found myself holding it in my hand!

Back at the hotel I packed the shoot into damp paper and polythene and posted it to the nursery for propagation. Being a rambler, the rose didn't come into flower until two years later. At its first flowering I consulted one or two knowledgeable rosarians, including Graham Stuart Thomas, as to what it might be. We all concluded that it was a rose called 'Gardenia', first introduced in 1899. It had been commercially extinct for some time prior to my finding it on Jersey. In 1990, after building up enough stock, we introduced 'Gardenia' to the world again, first asking permission of the original shoot's owners. They were happy to agree and, in exchange, I sent them a dozen rose bushes; a small token for an important rediscovery. As a matter of fact 'Gardenia' is still one of our best selling ramblers today. When this sort of thing happens and a rose as beautiful as this one is saved from extinction, I cannot help but wonder how it was allowed to disappear from rose growers' catalogues in the first place. Perhaps all gardeners and nurserymen are guilty of assuming that something new is always something better!

Much to my delight, both our children had by now joined the firm. Mandy had taken a two-year course at Burlingham Horticultural College and, in order to gain more experience, she spent a year or so afterwards at a well-known herbaceous plant nursery nearby. Richard, in turn, also attended Burlingham College then went on to take a landscape design course at Writtle College in Essex. They were now working full time at the nursery but their education continued. They were both taught how to bud roses and, of course, hybridising. Mandy showed a keen interest in this procedure and I asked her to take charge of the practical side of breeding new roses for the company. She took on her new role enthusiastically. The roses she has bred for us since then are proof of her success.

Richard, however, channelled his energies into design and began designing our exhibition stands as well as rose gardens for customers. He also took a keen interest in rose production.

It is never easy to be the boss's son, or daughter for that matter, in a small company like ours. They both had to withstand the inevitable teasing of the staff, a situation that all of us had to live with. I could hardly interfere. With the benefit of hindsight, all this paid off because they learned the most important lesson of all, man-management, and the warm and friendly relationship we enjoyed with our staff remained in place.

During the latter part of the 1980s the nursery flourished and our presence at shows played a big part in boosting our profile. The introduction of new roses was a big factor in attracting publicity. One new rose fro this period that stands out in my mind is 'Sir Frederick Ashton', named for the famous ballet dancer and choreographer at the request of the Queen Mother.

In the summer of 1986 Sir Frederick was staying at Sandringham House and was one of the royal party when it visited the Flower Show where we were exhibiting. I was showing the Queen Mother our roses when she looked straight at me and said 'Wouldn't it be nice if Sir Frederick had a rose named for him.' I took the hint and, by happy coincidence, my rose 'Anna Pavlova' provided us with a white sport that very summer. Because of the ballet connection it seemed right to call this sport 'Sir Frederick Ashton'.

I had been commissioned by the Prince of Wales and the Duke of Grafton to redesign the rose garden at Royal Lodge, Windsor. This was to be their present to the Queen Mother for her eighty-fifth birthday. It was a very cold, windy day in December when I first visited Royal Lodge to survey the rose garden. I was expecting to meet the head gardener but, to my surprise, the Queen Mother was there in person and we had tea and cakes together in her sitting room before venturing outside. She took me to see the garden herself, suitably dressed for the weather in a thick coat with a scarf around her head and fur-lined boots on her feet. I don't think this octogenarian actually felt the cold, although I confess that I was absolutely frozen. My instructions were to incorporate as many of her favourite roses into the planting scheme as I could. She had prepared a list of these for me. My plans were approved, and the following spring her gardeners planted the roses.

Roses don't enjoy growing in soil where other roses have previously grown, so one of the first things I advised was the removal of all the existing roses and the digging out by a mechanical digger of all the rose-sick soil, to a depth of 2 ft. New soil would then be brought in from another part of Windsor Park to replace the old soil. My basic design was simple and only marginally different from the original. Two long paths paved with York stone lead from end to end, with lateral paths dividing the area into four equal-sized beds, each holding about twenty roses. A tall beech hedge with two little seating alcoves protects the garden from the east and an equally tall conifer hedge forms the western boundary. Beneath this hedge I created a narrow border in which I planted a mixture of Species and Rugosa roses to add the extra interest of hips and colourful foliage to the garden in the autumn. The garden itself is sunken and can be viewed from the terrace above and, given that it is only about the size of a tennis court and totally enclosed, I tried to create the effect of a huge bowl of potpourri. This was done not only to provide an image to look down upon but as a tempting garden to walk into. To achieve this some of the roses would have to be planted closer together than would normally be the case and fragrance was an essential factor when selecting the varieties. For the two beds immediately below the terrace I chose to use older roses, mostly from the Victorian period, such as the lovely purple 'Reine des Violettes' and the sumptuous pinks 'Souvenir de la Malmaison' and 'Comte de Chambord'. For the two borders further from the terrace I selected modern roses, obviously these included the bright salmon 'Elizabeth of Glamis', the delicate pink 'Anna Pavlova' and the pure white 'Sir Frederick Ashton'. Finally, I decided to use lavender to edge all the borders.

I flew to Australia to participate in the Australian Heritage Rose Conference at Adelaide in November 1987. It was a good excuse to get away from the dull, cold November days in Norfolk for a while. During the Conference I met David Ruston for the first time. He owns an extensive rose garden at Renmark, 200 miles or so north of Adelaide. Having seen his roses on display at the Conference, it did not take much persuasion by him for me to agree to take a day out of my schedule to go to see his garden.

He drove us in his van overnight, taking me by the scenic route through South Australia. Early on in the journey, as we drove into the bush, we came upon a small homestead consisting of a little timber bungalow, old by Australian standards, which was almost completely covered by a tangled mass of roses of all types in full flower. Beside the front porch was a superb example of *Rosa indica* Major (soft pink), clearly once an understock that had shed the rose it had originally hosted sometime since. Neither David nor myself could resist knocking on the door to ask if we could take a look at the roses. The door was opened by a young lady who was startled to find two middle-aged men standing there. She told us that some years ago her father had bought a number of roses from a garden centre in Adelaide and that, sadly, soon after he had planted them he passed away. This meant that she had inherited the house and, with a young family to bring up, had left the roses to do their own thing. Since they had never been pruned and indeed had received no care at all, they had become gloriously entangled and were clearly enjoying their freedom. The last thing we said to her as we left was 'Please never buy any secateurs and let the roses continue to flourish by themselves.'

David had planned this route to enable me to see as much of Australia as possible before darkness fell. As the van ate up the miles, we swapped stories and tried to put the world to rights. We discovered that we had much more in common than just roses. He is a quintessential Australian with a keen sense of humour and a great love for his country. We got on like a house on fire and have remained good friends ever since. I vividly remember crossing the Murray River by ferry at sunset. It was one of the most intensely orange sunsets I had ever seen; highlighting the silhouettes of half a dozen or so inquisitive black swans looking for tasty titbits. We stopped here for a while to visit the pub beside the ferry. Cold beer and a packet of potato crisps each sustained us for the rest of the way.

The following day I spent several hours in David's delightful garden. He has amassed a huge collection of roses on the land that he inherited from his father. His father had emigrated to Australia from

England earlier in the century and was employed as an engineer specialising in irrigation at the nearby Murray river. His father had been a rose lover too and had installed a watering system in the garden using water pumped straight from the river. David's roses are exceptionally good because once a week throughout the hot Australian summer he uses his father's system and floods his land to a depth of three or four inches. I have an abiding memory of what is probably the biggest plant of the rose 'Mermaid' (sulphur yellow) in the world, supported by the tall, kangaroo-proof fence surrounding the garden.

In the evening David took me into the town of Renmark to catch the overnight bus to Sydney, a journey of about twenty-two hours. I slept through the first part of the night but when we reached Canberra we had a short break. Here I bought the worst fish and chips I have ever eaten in my life, made bearable with a bottle of Australian beer. The driver said we had thirty minutes so I set off to have a look at Government House. I think I was a little ambitious for, somehow, I managed to get lost, arriving back at the bus just as it was about to leave. On we went through Wagga Wagga to Sydney, arriving there about four in the afternoon. I was exhausted. When I finally reached my hotel, I fell into bed and managed to get a couple of hours' sleep.

I had planned to stay longer in Sydney but the excursion to David's garden in Renmark changed my plan, I now had only one evening here. Two of the staff of Harper Collins, the publishers of *Classic Roses* in Australia, gave up their evening to show me around. We took a pleasure boat ride around Sydney Harbour and the out-line of Sydney Bridge loomed tall and impressive in the moonlight. The Opera House was floodlit and although I had seen images of this building many times before, the reality was positively awe-inspiring. Later we dined in the revolving restaurant at the top of the Communications Tower and I could not tear my eyes away from the cyclorama of the city spread out below me. The next day I caught a plane to Christchurch, New Zealand; but I will write more about that country later.

Soon after the publication of *Classic Roses* my American publisher, through Christopher MacLehose, invited me to write a book

The Revd William Temple-Bourne
with his rose 'Uncle Bill', 1984

James Mason with his rose, 'James Mason',
Chelsea Flower Show, 1984

Patchy at Hargham

Approving pictures for *Classic Roses*

LEFT David Rushton, Renmark, South Australia, with the biggest example of
'Mermaid' in the world'! RIGHT The author with Peter Harkness in India

Carmine Russo's garden on Capri

Swangey Cottage, early 90s

Lord and Lady Walpole at Mannington Hall

The author with John and Norma Major before pandemonium ensued

Peter and Joan, Brooklyn Botanic Gardens

Introducing *Visions of Roses*

LEFT Skunks breakfasting in Kleine Lettunich's garden RIGHT The gardens at Ninfa

LEFT Joan, Laura, Alex and Oscar at Swangey Cottage
RIGHT Mr Eugene Yamada and his sister Miss Kay

Richard Beales and Mike Smithers with Ian and Tina Limmer (as Nelson and Lady Hamilton)

Visiting a rose garden in Japan

Meeting Princess Myoko in Japan

Introducing 'St Ethelburga' rose at St Ethelburga's Church with Prince Charles, the Bishop of London and Tom Gough

The author with Bishop Peter Nott and Princess Margaret introducing the 'Norwich Cathedral' rose

Debbie, Rachel Flood, Richard, Ken Flood and Amanda

The author with Queen Elizabeth at Chelsea, 1997

on Modern Roses. Anxious not to offend all the new-found devotees of old roses by putting my name to a book on modern roses, I at first declined. Christopher, however, came up with a compromise that was acceptable to both the Americans and myself. This was to cover the entire twentieth century of roses, including not only the Hybrid Teas and Floribundas but the Hybrid Musks and older Ramblers and Climbers. When published, I thought it looked and read like a desirable book but, for some reason, it did not sell as well as *Classic Roses*. Perhaps it was aimed at a different section of the book market or, could it have been fractionally overpriced? I dip into its pages from time to time but I do not get quite the same amount of satisfaction with this book as I still do with my first one.

My next trip abroad, in spring 1988, was to Bermuda to speak at the North American Rose Conference there. On arrival the thing that struck me most was the island's apparent 'Britishness'. I went back later that same year to deliver another lecture, this time to the Bermudan Rose Society. About halfway through my stay the island was hit by a hurricane. Only once before had I experienced such a ferocious wind and that was in the great October storm back in England when so many trees were lost and buildings damaged. Bermuda is far better equipped to cope with such a storm but to experience it personally was very exhilarating.

Over the last two or three hundred years of Bermuda's history settlers, and even those just passing through on their way to America, took roses to the island. Such is the climate there that all plants, including roses, have no dormant season. If a rose is constantly in flower, or only gets a short time of rest each year, mutations can easily occur in its genetic make up, some distinctly, others discreetly. This phenomenon may result in a rose becoming no longer recognisable as the variety first taken to the island. There are about ten such mystery roses growing on Bermuda. These have been given names by the members of the Bermuda Rose Society, names such as 'Smith's Parish' (pink and white bicolour) indicating where it was found, and 'Miss Atwood' (apricot) after the lady who originally discovered it.

I suppose that one of the most significant events that happened at the nursery in the late 1980s was the acquisition of our first computer – by today's standards a clumsy-looking machine, which I believe was called a Commodore. The first thing we used it for was stock control, then wages. By the beginning of the 1990s we had started to operate an all-singing all-dancing system. I now take computers for granted but have always avoided learning how to use them. Although they pull my leg about this, I am fortunate that my staff and those around me seem to be wizards at it. It simply means that I do not have to learn any new tricks at my time of life.

13

Roses, Cacti and Chapatis

Soon after publication of the Italian translation of *Classic Roses*, I received a telephone call from a Neapolitan pasta maker, Carmine Russo. In charming broken English he invited me to Naples, from where he would take me to his weekend villa on Capri. He wanted me to help him design a rose garden there. A few days later Joan and I were met at Naples Airport by Carmine who took us to the harbour where we boarded a ferry for Capri. The taxi ride to his villa through a maze of narrow streets, uphill all the way, was quite hair-raising.

When we reached the villa, situated on the side of a hill with stunning views across the island to the Bay of Naples, the first thing Carmine did was to show me his garden. It was no bigger than a tennis court and I was amazed to see that it was already full of sizeable cacti. Carmine soon made it clear to me that, under no circumstances, were these prickly succulents to be disturbed and that the varieties of roses I selected would be planted amongst them. For roses to be able to survive in the heat of a Capri summer they would need regular irrigation and, bearing in mind that the villa was only occupied at weekends, an automatic watering system had to be installed.

I went back to plant the roses a few weeks later and followed this up with a visit by both of us early the next year. The roses loved the automatic watering but the cacti loved it even more, and I found that both the genera had doubled in size. Clearly these two ill-matched groups had formed an alliance and seemed to have every intention of living together in close embrace. Whilst there, Joan and I spent some happy hours enjoying the island. We especially enjoyed Ana Capri and the Villa of San Michele, high above the Bay of Naples. We managed to extend our stay once back in Naples itself and visited Pompeii.

The year following our visit to Capri I went to Lucknow in India to speak at a rose conference. The jumbo jet I was booked on left Heathrow fourteen hours late. On arrival at New Delhi Airport I found a scruffy-looking Indian gentleman holding up a placard bearing my name, misspelled as 'Beles'. He seemed to be deaf or something for we had great difficulty understanding each other. He took me by the arm to one of the many taxis vying for business outside the airport. When we were ready to drive off the taxi driver, who spoke a little English, asked me where I wanted to go. I had not been told where I was to stay only that I was to be met at the airport.

It turned out that my escort did not know either, he was a substitute for the person who had long since given up waiting for me due to my late arrival. My escort and the taxi driver then put their heads together and told me that they had decided to take me to the Indian Institute of Floriculture. I later discovered that this was where my escort worked as a gardener.

After what seemed ages driving through unlit roads, we reached the Institute and I was shown into one of the student rooms. Clearly I was in for a completely new experience. The bed was a single one, with a grubby mattress. Suspended from four posts, one at each corner of the bed, was a tatty mosquito net. In one corner of the room was a dirty white enamel bucket and, on a washstand, a jug of water which of course I dared not drink. The only window was long and narrow and, in order to see out, I had to stand on tiptoe. A single light bulb of no more than 30 watts hung from a cord in the centre of the room.

After showing me to the room my escort shuffled off without a word. Soon I heard the rustling of leaves and noises from some form of wildlife coming from outside the window. I confess to having felt quite scared. There was no key to lock the door. There was no chair in the room so I laid my anorak on the mattress, pulled the mosquito net around my shoulders and sat on the bed, with my back to the wall. I felt grubby and itchy from imaginary fleas but eventually managed to fall asleep (hardly surprising, as I had not had any sleep in the last twenty-four hours). At dawn I was woken by screeching peacocks and barking dogs and soon I heard movement outside the door. I was so thirsty and hungry by now that I decided to investigate and find some food.

I eventually found myself in what was obviously a dining room where young men dressed in white, presumably students, were having breakfast. They seemed taken aback to see me and, after their initial surprise, totally ignored me. Seeing a large brown enamel teapot on a table close by I picked up a mug and helped myself, hoping that the water had been boiled. The tea was very strong and I had to drink it without milk or sugar. I was feeling very conspicuous but pushed my way in to take what I took to be a chapati from a pile that had clearly been freshly baked. I do not know what else it could have been but it had a rubbery texture and little or no flavour. After this meagre breakfast I took a walk outside in the garden.

Early morning mist hung amongst the trees and several monkeys were sitting watching me with curiosity, some from the ground, others on the walls, scratching themselves. It all seemed very Kiplingesque and I found myself looking around for a tiger. Grazing on what passed for a lawn were a couple of sacred cows.

I was desperately anxious and had no way of knowing what, if anything, was going to happen next. I had horrible visions of being stranded here and I didn't even know if my 'guide' of the previous evening had notified anyone of my arrival. The students, all male, were not even talking amongst themselves and I decided that they would not be able to help. It was almost as though they were part of some silent order. I found a toilet of sorts and then returned to my room and dozed off again. After about an hour a knock came on the door and two well-dressed young Indians in western suits blustered in. They spoke good English and were full of apologies. They took me to a waiting limousine. Apparently I should have been taken to the house of the Indian Rose Society's President the previous evening. When I finally arrived at his house I received VIP treatment and, thankfully, was able to indulge in a long hot soak, the first bath I had had since I left home. I had gone from the ridiculous to the sublime overnight.

Later that day I was scheduled to fly from Delhi to Lucknow but to add to the already bizarre situation, Air India pilots were on a one-day strike. This meant that I could look forward to a good night's sleep and rather than loaf about in my now salubrious surroundings I asked one of the servants to arrange for a car and driver to take me around Old Delhi. This was a salutary experience. I had never seen such poverty in my life. My driver wore a turban so I assumed he was a Sikh. He spoke a little English and turned out to be quite a good guide. The car and driver cost me the equivalent of five pounds in rupees for the whole of that afternoon. When I paid him, I gave him double the amount, the extra as a tip. He was taken aback and, at first, would not take it. When I insisted, he told me that he had a wife and three children to support and that I had just given him the equivalent of a normal month's pay. I felt disturbed by this and I tell this story only because when I related it to my hosts at dinner that evening they reprimanded me for being so generous.

The next morning I boarded a plane, arriving at Lucknow in time for lunch. I presented my lecture that afternoon. It would appear that the Indian Rose Society, on hearing of the flight delays, had simply postponed the Conference until I arrived. Also speaking at this Conference was another Englishman, Peter Harkness of Harkness Nurseries, and we were both guests of a charming Indian family. The patriarch of this family, Mr Agawal, was a lovable and interesting character. He was obviously an educated man and very well read. Because he was stone deaf, conversation with him was difficult. However, he spoke excellent English and could lip-read with little or no effort. Apparently as a young man he had been a close follower of Gandhi. He enjoyed reciting Shakespeare to us. With him, lived his son and daughter-in-law and their two children, a boy and a girl aged about eight and ten. The family owned a rose nursery and Peter and I were fascinated by their production methods that, to say the least, were primitive compared to those of the West. There seemed to be workers everywhere and we learned that most of them were relatives of the Agawals. It is quite normal, I believe, for small businesses in India to employ as many members of their extended family as they can. Peter and I thoroughly enjoyed staying with this close-knit Indian family and sharing in their way of life.

Although Peter and I are both rose growers, we were taken to the annual Lucknow Chrysanthemum Show where, as guests of honour, we were garlanded with chains of chrysanthemums. Peter was given the job of declaring the show open and I was asked to present the prizes at the end. This went on for over an hour, with every single exhibitor being awarded a prize or certificate. My stay in India was all too short but I will never forget it.

At last, in May 1989, we won our first gold medal at Chelsea Flower Show. We were all ecstatic and celebrated in style that evening. That year our stand was innovative, as Richard had designed it as a garden, with wide pathways under arches and alongside a trellis, allowing visitors to walk through and enjoy the roses and their perfume close up. This was much appreciated and I believe ours was the first nursery ever at Chelsea to allow our customers access to the roses for them to browse to their hearts' content.

It was about now that something happened that I now look back on with a mixture of embarrassment and amusement. One Saturday morning, on my way to the nursery from Hall Farmhouse, I came upon what seemed to me to be a headless body lying prone on the grass verge underneath a large tree. This particular part of the road ran through what is known locally as Hargham Woods, the whole area being a bit on the spooky side. I stopped my car and looked with some trepidation at the motionless form. It still did not move and, steeling myself, I got out of the car and moved closer. The 'corpse' appeared to be male with the top half of his torso covered by a large, black bin liner. The remainder was covered by a black polythene sheet. Sticking out from under the sheet was a foot, with a large hole in the heel of a grubby sock. 'Don't touch this,' I said to myself, 'call the police.'

These were the days before mobile phones so I drove quickly to the nursery, just up the road, and telephoned the local police station; telling them that I had found what I thought was a dead body – headless at that. I arranged to wait for them at the scene. When the two policemen turned up, one of them went over to the 'body', studied it and poked it with his foot. The 'corpse' sat up, removed his plastic wrapping, sniffed, glared at the three of us and ambled off, muttering under his breath. It turned out that the police knew this tramp and were forever moving him on. I still see one of these policemen from time to time and he cannot resist teasing me a little about my 'headless body'.

In November that year I flew to Texas to participate in a get together of classic roses devotees at the gardens of the Antique Rose

Emporium, Brenham, a rose nursery owned by Mike and Jean Shoup. They took me to a dance hall one evening and my hosts tried to teach me the Texan Two Step. I should have told them that I have two left feet! On another day we had lunch in a Texan roadhouse. Everyone here drove a pick up truck and both the men and the gals were dressed as cowboys, with spurs on their boots and 'ten gallon' Stetsons on their heads. The steaks they were eating were as big as their hats. I think I was the only customer in the roadhouse who ordered fish.

I knew of course that 'everything in Texas is big' but I hadn't realised just how big and I will never forget a thunderstorm I experienced in that state. It came in the middle of the night and the lightning was brighter and more frequent and the claps of thunder louder than any storm I had previously experienced, including the one in Bermuda.

My hosts had arranged for me to take two days out to visit the headquarters of the American Rose Society in Shreveport, Louisiana. This involved quite a long drive through what I was told was Davy Crockett country in central and northern Texas. During the drive I was able to relax and take in the scenery. It always surprises me what little traffic there is when out on the open country roads of America. We drove through heavily wooded countryside and the trees, in keeping with everything else in Texas, are huge compared with those I know in Norfolk.

14

A New Abode, New Directors and a Secret Garden

Early in 1990 we moved from the farmhouse to a smaller cottage about two miles away. We had mixed feelings about this but, in truth, we no longer needed such a large house. We realised something was brewing when one morning our landlord telephoned and asked if he could come to see us. When he arrived he explained that he had a smaller house vacant on the estate and that he really needed our farmhouse for his son, who wanted to move back to Norfolk.

When we went to look at the cottage we took to it straightaway. It is situated in an idyllic part of the Hargham Estate, adjacent to woodland and is reached by driving down a long track across fields. There is only one other house nearby, a small farmhouse. The cottage is very old and quite picturesque with beams and differing levels to the ceilings. We agreed to move in.

We were downsizing substantially and there was insufficient room in Swangey Cottage to accommodate all the furniture, paintings and bric-a-brac we had accumulated after fifteen years of living in a large house. In the event it gave us a good opportunity to dispose of a lot of junk, store the furniture we could no longer use and start again. We soon settled in and really loved living there. It had two wood-burning stoves for heating and, as back up, the two large living rooms had night storage heaters. In spite of this the draughts came whistling through every nook and cranny, of which there were many, from ill-fitting doors and windows. It was very difficult to keep the cottage warm in winter but, in summer, it was heavenly living there.

We loved the flora and fauna but not the grey squirrels because, despite our making it difficult for them, they ate all the food we put out for the plentiful wild birds. A pair of jackdaws regularly built their nest in the chimneypot of the unused kitchen chimney and each summer a very noisy colony of pipistrelle bats also shared our house with us, living up in the attic. Every evening, at dusk, we enjoyed watching them swooping around for insects. Where they went to in the winter we have no idea. The estate had a gamekeeper and raised its own pheasants. These roamed freely in our garden until such time as they met their fate when the shooting season began. I find it difficult to come to terms with how shooting semi-tame birds, even when in flight, can be considered a sport. In the woods adjacent to our cottage, wild roe deer and muntjacs nervously grazed this woodland wilderness.

By now the three acres of gardens I had designed and planted at the Attleborough Nurseries were almost mature and are becoming very important as a shop window for our roses. The garden as a whole is divided into five outdoor rooms, which in turn are subdivided by rose hedges and walkways and pergolas, with the open spaces within each 'room' taken up by lawns. It is a fundamental rule in my garden designs to include open spaces because I believe that gardens are not just about the plants therein but also the people who enjoy them. The first of the 'rooms' came into being soon after we arrived at Attleborough and this area is devoted to displaying our full collection of Hybrid Musk roses and lots of different Rugosas. On the western boundary to our car park I planted a long hedge of the beautiful carmine Rugosa 'Roseraie de l'Hay'. On warm summer days and evenings this lovely rose wafts out a distinct fragrance of cloves and in the autumn becomes a mass of tawny gold foliage. The Hybrid Musks in this 'room' form a single bed underplanted with a variety of herbaceous plants and herbs. These include several different varieties of peonies and quite a range of grey foliage plants such as Senecio, Lavender, Phlomis and Nepita. Rising at intervals from the border of pastel-coloured Hybrid Musks are a number of obelisks, on which are growing such delightful, unusual varieties of climbing roses as 'Cupid' (soft pink) and 'Phyllis Bide' (pink to copper). Also on these obelisks are a few ramblers of sympathetic colours to the Hybrid Musks beneath them, such as 'François Juranville' (shrimp pink) and 'Blush Noisette' (mauve-coloured). The border at the southern end of this 'room' is defined by a tall beech hedge, on the north side of which is a wide border of shade-tolerant varieties of roses (the sun drops behind this hedge from midday onwards in high summer). The shade-tolerant roses are mostly Gallicas. I wanted this end of the 'room' to be made up of red and purple shades, of which there are many amongst the Gallicas. Included here are 'Tuscany Superb', 'La Belle Sultane', 'Charles de Mills' and 'Alain Blanchard'. Scattered amongst these roses are more grey-foliaged herbaceous plants.

Stepping through the beech hedge by way of a tall arch covered with a very large plant of the soft pink 'Paul's Himalayan Musk', one comes to the second of the five 'rooms'. Cut into the lawns here are some informal beds containing a large mixture of roses and a wide variety of herbaceous plants. The east side of this area of the garden is devoted to some of the old Tea roses and a few China roses. These include such Victorian favourites as 'Maman Cochet' (soft pink), 'Belle Lyonnaise' (soft yellow) and 'Blush Noisette' (lavender pink). Amongst the Chinas mixed in with the Teas are 'Arethusa' (soft orange), 'Cécille Brunner' (pale pink), and 'Perle d'Or' (coppery yellow). On the southern border is a collection of ancient varieties of Gallicas, Damasks, Centifolias and Moss Roses of mostly pink shades, including 'Empress Josephine' growing arm in arm with 'Chapeau de Napoléon'. Next door to these two is the ancient Damask rose 'York and Lancaster', its flowers a mixture of pink and white. This rose is thought to have inspired an unknown fifteenth-century heraldic artist to create the symbolic Tudor Rose emblem. It is interesting that this famous emblem has lasted as a brand for almost 550 years.

Moving further along the southern border, there is a wide arch-way covered with the very vigorous foundling rose 'Sir Cedric Morris', a foundling because it was discovered as a seedling in his garden by Sir Cedric Morris, the famous artist. Mentioning his name takes me back to an evening in July 1979 when, at his request, I drove to his home in Hadleigh in Suffolk to see his new discovery. I arrived at his house about half an hour late to be met by an irate housekeeper, angry because I was late for dinner. With no prelimi-naries we sat down at the pine kitchen table to eat. A sort of stroganoff was ladled on to wooden platters and I ate it simply to be polite, as it was hardly the most appetising meal I had ever eaten. I dared not leave any as I was terrified of the housekeeper. It wasn't long before I realised that my host was almost blind. During this repast Sir Cedric told me how he had found the seedling and how he hoped I would introduce it for him. Once we had finished eating, the housekeeper, who had not spoken during the meal, took Sir Cedric's arm and gestured for me to follow them into the garden. By now it was dusk but, even so, it was easy to see the rose because it was enormous and was covered in masses of small, sweetly-scented, single white flowers. I knew from the moment I saw this rose that I wanted to introduce it and it has now become a favourite in our collection of vigorous scramblers.

Back to our own gardens, there are three tall, beautiful cedar trees, randomly planted at about twenty feet apart, taking up most of the space in the lawn on the west side of this 'room'. They are now about twenty years old and each one is about thirty feet tall but they will of course get much bigger as time goes on. I am very proud of these trees. They were originally given to me as tiny little bonsai at Chelsea Flower Show to thank me for a favour I had done for her by a bonsai specialist. While I can appreciate the skill and dedication required in growing and nurturing bonsai trees I personally feel that this art is akin to the old Oriental practice of binding children's feet to keep them small. Consequently, the first thing I did when I brought the little trees back to my garden was to release them from their torture and plant them in the ground. I swear that every time I walk past these trees I can hear a whisper of thanks in the breeze as it passes through their branches.

Moving towards the south, through the archway of 'Sir Cedric Morris', we enter the third 'room' of the garden. This is split into two parts. On the east side, beds of roses are arranged formally around a central bed, in the middle of which is a stone feature of a pineapple on a plinth. The roses here are made up of three varieties, 'Bonica' – pink, 'Twenty-Fifth' – red and 'Macmillan Nurse' – creamy-white. The west side of this 'room' is a large, open lawn with seating where visitors can linger for a while as they take in the beauty of the gardens. To add an extra dimension to this garden we have built a pergola, covered in rambling roses, from north to south straight down the middle. A few years ago the local Amateur

Dramatic Society, of which my wife is a member, performed *A Midsummer Night's Dream* on Midsummer's Night in this garden with the roses as a backdrop.

Dividing this 'room' from the next is a long tunnel of roses, stretching from east to west, with openings for access at either end and in the middle This tunnel is adorned with fifty or so different climbers and ramblers which, when in full flower, are quite spectacular. Still moving in a southerly direction, to the other side of the rose tunnel, one steps into the fourth and largest of the five 'rooms' making up the garden. Here the lawns are more undulating than in any other part of the garden and five island beds of roses are scattered throughout. As well as roses these beds are composed of a wide variety of perennials and bulbous plants. However, the most significant feature is a large footbridge that straddles a sizeable pond full of koi carp and goldfish. I find it very therapeutic standing on this bridge watching the fish swimming around in the crystal clear water beneath me.

The final 'room' consists of two long borders running from east to west on either side of a grass walkway. These borders contain the majority of our Species Collection and, while the flowering season of these roses is short, when in bloom they make a stunning sight. In the autumn however the beds are a riot of different-coloured foliage and berries of all shapes and sizes. I love these rose gardens because they give so much pleasure to both myself and all our visitors every year. My business is no different from any other from a management point of view but I am fortunate that the end product has its compensations.

The American publishers of my books *Classic Roses* and *Twentieth-Century Roses* decided it would be a worthwhile exercise to publish the two together as one book. In the winter of 1991/92 I merged the roses from each book into their correct chronological order; easier said than done. It was time-consuming and arduous for I also added an extra 300 varieties and species of roses to the combined volume. Entitled *Roses*, the book was in the shops by November 1992 and received several satisfying reviews.

Mentioning satisfying reviews I must comment on Mandy's books. *Old Fashioned Roses*, her first, had been published a year or so prior to this and I felt very proud that my daughter had followed in my footsteps, as it were. It was well received both here in England and in America. Since then she has written three other books: *Roses – A Care Manual*, *Rose Basics* and her latest, *Roses, A Colour Guide*, which has just been published. Richard was responsible for photographing a fair number of the roses for this book.

For some time we had been trying to get permission from the Norfolk Highways Department and Breckland District Council to put up some Tourist Board signs to point the way to our nurseries from the A11 trunk road. In order to get these we had to prove that we had a substantial number of visitors each year. We took the advice of the East Anglian Tourist Board and started a visitors' book. After about a year we realised what a useful aid this had turned out to be. We were agreeably surprised to discover that, in that year, we had visitors from no less than twenty-five different countries. We eventually obtained permission for the signs but still keep up the visitors' book. One afternoon a Chinese couple came to the nursery and Ian made sure they signed the book, hoping for an address in China. When they had gone he checked their entry to find that they had written 'Mr and Mrs Tom, Chinese Fish and Chip Shop, Attleborough'!

Mandy was now married and our first grandchild, a little girl called Laura, was born in January 1992, when the snowdrops were just peeping through the frozen ground. Richard was still living with us at Swangey Cottage. At that time I was very busy at the nursery so I made both Mandy and Richard directors so that they could share some of the responsibility. The July following Laura's birth was a sad month because we lost Uncle Ted, whom I had always looked up to. Ted had been my staunch ally and friend for many years.

At Chelsea Flower Show 1993 we introduced a rose called 'John Grooms' for the charity of that name. The launch however was quite a fiasco. Norma Major, the then Prime Minister's wife, came to the stand to receive the rose on behalf of the charity. This was at a time when John Major was experiencing some political difficulties. There was much talk about sleaze and some of his own party, the Conservatives, had attempted to plot his downfall. He had just challenged them 'to put up or shut up'. To our great surprise John Major accompanied his wife to our stand attended by a bevy of security men. Within seconds pandemonium broke out, as what seemed like hundreds of paparazzi appeared from nowhere. They were all over our stand, trampling down the roses and swinging from the trellis in order to get 'the photograph'. In the ensuing bedlam Mandy was pushed roughly into the display and one over-enthusiastic photographer had to be physically removed from the marquee by the security men. Later the Majors sent a message of apology for the chaos they had inadvertently caused.

When all had quietened down, we only had minutes to repair the stand before the judges came to do their rounds. Until all this happened we had been optimistic about winning a gold medal but, thanks to the paparazzi, not a chance! In the event the judges gave us a silver gilt medal but the publicity engendered more than made up for not getting the gold.

Vivian Russell approached me in the summer of that year, to make a video of Old Roses; this was to be her debut as a film-maker and she suggested we call it 'A Celebration of Old Roses'. She had been a customer of ours for some time and had fallen head over heels in love with the classic roses, buying hundreds for her garden in the Lake District.

Her idea was to film the story of the older roses; something I myself had wanted to do for some time. She provided the finance for the film whilst I provided the setting, the roses and the story line. The main setting for the video was Elsing Hall near Dereham, Norfolk. The Elizabethan house is surrounded by an ancient moat and with its garden, famous for the large collection of old and historical roses, is situated in the middle of farmland and has bags of atmosphere. The present house replaced a much earlier one and I came to love the feeling of history that emanates from this place. At an earlier period of its life it had been owned by the Hastings family, who were Keepers of Horse for Edward, the Black Prince; many of their charges must have taken part in the Battle of Crécy.

During the latter part of the 1980s I had been in discussion with Lord Walpole of Mannington Hall in north Norfolk. Mannington is a delightful medieval manor house, with its gardens open to the public. It was Lord and Lady Walpole's idea to plant up the old walled kitchen garden with a historic collection of roses and we were asked to supply the plants. The new garden was to be laid out chronologically, starting with the medieval roses at the entrance and working through various different sections for each period to the modern roses situated at the end of the walk.

Robin and Laurel Walpole developed a keen interest in roses and have become experts in their own right. After some discussion it was decided that an alliance should be formed between us. We were always glad of extra capital and this idea seemed a good way of expanding the business. The plan was to grow roses commercially on Robin's farmland and he would sell some of them at Mannington. However, growing roses some forty miles away from Attleborough soon proved uneconomic, so we stopped doing so.

While all this was happening, my half-sister Rosie decided to give up pig farming at Buck Brigg and thus released land on which she could grow roses. I had already taught her how to bud during the Swardeston days so all she needed now were lessons on the process of growing roses. With regular visits from Ian, our Manager, she started growing about 20,000 bushes for us each year. She found growing roses far more lucrative than pig farming and she, too, fell in love with them. She started a small retail North Norfolk branch of Peter Beales' Roses. In time Rosie, helped by my mother, created a superb rose garden at Buck Brigg.

Early in the 1990s I became a 'Holder of the National Collection of Rosa Species'. This was recognition by the Royal Horticultural Society and the National Council for the Preservation of Plants and Gardens that my collection of Species roses is the most comprehensive in the country, composed as it is of over 100 different wild roses, that is to say 'nature's pure roses'. This type of rose is widely distributed in the Northern Hemisphere and we have examples from the Himalayas, the Middle East, North America and Europe. Becoming custodian of this collection was important to me because, ever since I first became involved with roses, the wild roses of the world have been close to my heart.

To some gardeners Species roses are seen as rather esoteric and, except in large collections, are seldom used in modern gardens. I find this sad because they make ideal flowering shrubs, seldom looking out of place in shrubberies and herbaceous borders, not to mention wild or woodland gardens where space permits. Another reason why they tend to be overlooked by modern garden designers is that they have a relatively short flowering period. What they tend to forget is that, almost without exception, Species roses bear an abundance of hips of all shapes, colours and sizes throughout autumn and winter and these can be quite dramatic in appearance in midwinter, as well as providing tasty meals for birds and other wildlife. Most Species are very thorny and adapt readily as hedging plants and some of the more vigorous forms, if planted strategically, can be a useful deterrent to burglars. I always try to incorporate a few Species roses into my garden designs to add that little 'difference', almost as a signature to my work.

I flew to New Zealand in 1990 to speak at an International Heritage Rose Conference at Christchurch. Roses are very popular in New Zealand and I am on record as saying 'There are more rose bushes in this country than sheep.' Wherever I went I found gardens overflowing with superb roses. One such garden was owned by a good friend, Trevor Griffiths, whom I had previously met with his wife Dixie when he visited England. Trevor also owned a flourishing rose nursery. After the conference Nigel Pratt, a rose nurseryman whom I know very well, drove me 200 miles north to Nelson where he and his wife Judy have their nursery. Their son Ben, at that time, was staying with us in England and gaining experience at our nursery. Nigel and Judy's business is called Tasman Bay Roses. They had grown lots of our rose varieties for several years and it was because of this that Ben decided he would like to come to us to improve his knowledge. He lived with us and became very much a part of the family. He planned to stay with us for a year but it turned into three.

Never before had I designed a 'secret garden' but in the spring of 1992 a lady called Gerd Perkins from Plumpton, near Lewes in Sussex invited me to visit her for this very purpose. The site she had chosen nestled discreetly within the grounds of her small estate and was enclosed by tall beech hedges. She was Norwegian and had an American husband. They had bought Plumpton Place, a Lutyens house, a few years earlier. She wanted me to provide a planting plan for her 'secret garden' almost overnight. She was clearly in a hurry to get on with it. She really loved roses and, I discovered, knew quite a lot about them. I'm afraid our relationship became rather strained. Her need for haste irritated me and I could so easily have told her to do it herself. Thankfully, as it turned out, I refrained from doing so.

In the autumn, when all the planting in the 'secret garden' had been completed, Gerd invited Joan and me to dinner and to stay the night at Plumpton Place. It was at dinner that one of her friends, also a guest, told us that our hostess was suffering from terminal cancer. Everything then fell into place and I felt extremely guilty for even considering telling her to do it herself. Gerd lived long enough to see her roses flower in their first summer in her 'secret garden' and I learned a valuable lesson, to be more tolerant.

Pashley Manor had always been on my list of 'houses and gardens to visit', so it was no hardship to go there at the invitation of James and Angela Sellick the following spring to discuss ways in which our two businesses could work together. The gardens at Pashley Manor are open to the public every summer and it was decided that the Sellicks would inaugurate an annual Rose Weekend. This involved our putting up a small stand of roses and sending a member of staff to man it and do a 'Garden Walk and Talk' about roses. The first weekend was a great success and we have been attending Pashley Manor Rose Weekend ever since.

We received an invitation in 1993 to attend a Garden Party at Buckingham Palace. Our names had been put forward by the Head Gardener of the Sandringham Estate, Fred Waite, to mark our many years of exhibiting at the Sandringham Flower Show. This was an occasion for dressing up but I confess I felt very conspicuous walking down the Mall, wearing my morning suit and carrying my top hat. There were thousands of other guests there and we didn't meet any of the Royals. We did enjoy the gardens and loved the pink flamingos; however after the buffet, when it came time for us to have coffee, they had run out of cups and saucers!

15

Concrete Jungle, A Boa Constrictor and Lots of Ghosts

The video 'A Celebration of Old Roses' had been very well received. However some of those who bought it felt that it should have included more practical footage, such as pruning. Consequently, in the summer of 1993, we set about making another. For this video a partnership was formed between a television cameraman, Tony Aldous, a producer, Tim Curtis, and myself and was to be filmed with a digital camera (the previous one had been filmed with a movie camera). The video 'Growing Roses with Peter Beales' was ready for sale at Christmas 1994.

Mike Lowe, a rose grower from Nashua, New Hampshire, had visited our nursery some years before and, with his wife Irene, had stayed for a couple of days. At that time they invited us to stay with them in America and we went there in June 1994. Richard came with us and drove our hired car from Boston Airport. It was one of the hottest days New England had experienced for many years. Coupled with the high humidity, the heat was certainly greater than we had ever experienced, with temperatures well into the high 30s centigrade. The lecture took place in Mike's garden that afternoon and several of the audience, especially the elderly ladies, had to shelter from the baking sun under nearby trees. This visit though was not only memorable for the heat but for a reason in no way related to roses. It was the day that O. J. Simpson was arrested after a long car-chase, which we watched with incredulity on American television. From Nashua the three of us set off to visit Cape Cod, see the sights and relax.

On another occasion when visiting the Lowes, Mike drove Joan and me the 300 or so miles to New York, stopping off for a while at Attleboro, our namesake town in Massachusetts. I was going to

New York to lecture at the Cranford Rose Garden, part of Brooklyn Botanical Gardens, then managed by Stephen Scanniello the rose curator. I enjoyed this garden which is memorable for its large collection of older Hybrid Tea roses.

Brooklyn Botanical Gardens are situated in the middle of an urban concrete jungle, in a part of New York known for its high crime rate. The Rose Garden has become a backyard for many people of many races; a patch of colour and fragrance to those who have no gardens of their own. Seeing the pleasure experienced by these visitors proved to me that roses are therapeutic as well as ornamental and, in my anonymity there, I felt a sense of pride knowing that my profession was capable of giving so much joy to so many.

1995 was quite a year. Our grandson Alex was born in August and, just before this happy event, I was inducted into the Livery of the Worshipful Company of Gardeners, becoming at the same time a Freeman of the City of London. It was good to join the Gardeners Company as it satisfied my strong sense of history. They received their Charter from James I in 1605 and their membership is still as strong as ever. During that spring I also became President of the Norfolk and Norwich Horticultural Society for the year.

The remainder of that year was spent visiting the various gardens to be featured in my next book, *Visions of Roses*. I had come to know Vivian Russell quite well during the making of the video and we decided we would do a book on rose gardens together; I would write the text and Vivian would take the photographs. This book would feature rose gardens that had not previously been written up extensively in other publications. There would be a total of thirty-two gardens in all, fourteen in the UK, ten in the USA, four in France and four in Italy.

Vivian went ahead of me to take the photographs when the gardens were at their best. It was not so important for me to see the gardens while the roses were in flower; I could visit them at my convenience. The British gardens were covered by half a dozen or so long weekends spent in various parts of the country. This is not the place to discuss each of the gardens, but I will pick out a few of the more interesting ones.

A natural choice was the rose garden at Royal Lodge, Windsor, mentioned earlier. One of the pictures Vivian took in this garden was of the Dolls' House, a small-scale replica of a thatched Welsh cottage presented to the Queen, then Princess Elizabeth, on her sixth birthday, with the rose 'The Queen Mother' growing in front of it.

Another was the rose garden at Hambleden Manor near Henley-on-Thames that I had been commissioned to design and plant by Lady Hambleden in the late 1980s. The garden had matured and the roses looked really superb. Visiting it for the first time since its completion made me feel good as it was obvious that all the features I had incorporated in the design had worked.

I had envisaged creating a rose garden as it would have been laid out in Victorian times. Although the Manor House had been built of flint and brick in the early seventeenth century, changes had been made to the building during the nineteenth century. I settled on the soft lines of a circular wheel-like plan, with a round central bed as the hub and each bed thereafter separated into borders by paths radiating outwards with no one path opposite another. It was to be purely and simply a rose garden for easy maintenance. No other types of plants were used, not even bulbs or edging plants around the beds. The beds were defined in cottage garden style with flint stones set into the soil. Some eighty varieties of roses were selected and care was taken not to have contrasting shades growing in the same beds. Except for the more strident colours, the whole spectrum of colour was used. For maximum effect three to five of each variety were grouped together and, although consideration was given to ultimate sizes, the objective was to achieve an overall undulating effect, avoiding any semblance of uniformity. Without exception all the roses used would have been known to the Victorians. The centre bed was planted with pastel-coloured Hybrid Musks, with the Weeping Standard rose 'Félicité Perpétue' (creamy-white) as a centrepiece, trained as an umbrella. Walking through the garden now one can brush against roses overhanging the path and take in the perfume that pervades the air all around. The Manor House is situated at the point where the land starts to rise out of the Thames Valley and, as one drives through the picturesque little village of Hambleden and climbs the hill towards the house, the rose garden can be clearly seen in all its glory.

Of the American gardens featured in my book, the following stand out in my mind. First, the Long Island garden owned by Martha Stewart, the well-known American life-style writer and TV personality. Her roses at Lily Pond Avenue are some of the best I have seen in America and the garden was designed on English lines. I did not meet her but was given the freedom of her garden. The second garden worth mentioning here is memorable more because of the personality of its owner than the roses that, frankly, were disappointing. 'I have always wanted to be a landscaper, gardening has been my lifelong passion,' she said, explaining that she had also gardened in England, the Cotswolds to be precise. She was Lee Radziwill, sister of Jackie Kennedy.

The third garden I visited on Long Island was that owned by Robert Dash, an artist who was famous for drawing and painting the male form. I was somewhat taken aback when Dash asked me into the house, via his studio. Drawings of nude males and phallic symbols covered the walls and much more of his work along similar lines could be found throughout the house. It took me a while to acclimatise to all this. After Dash had shown me around his garden he offered to take me out to dinner and we went to a very high-class restaurant in one of the Hamptons. During the meal the conversation came round to my video 'A Celebration of Old Roses'. Sitting at the next table was a very attractive blonde, in her mid-twenties I would guess, accompanied by an older lady who Dash told me later was probably her mother. While we were talking about the video, the blonde siren started to flirt with me to the point where it became obvious to Bob Dash because he suddenly said 'Am I in the way?' At the same time the blonde wiggled across to our table and asked me if I was a film producer. 'No, just a gardener,' I replied, at which she took her companion's arm and moved to another part of the restaurant.

Another American garden that I remember well is at Santa Cruz, California and belongs to a gregarious lady called Kleine Lettunich. I was introduced to this garden and Kleine by Bill Grant, a distinguished Californian rose devotee who has since become a good friend. The roses in Kleine's garden are superb. The garden is situated on the side of a hill and therefore very dry; liberal irrigation helps the roses to flourish. Kleine has a number of unusual pets including tortoises, parrots, rabbits, goats and bantams, not to mention the semi-tame skunks that breakfast every morning on cat food pellets on her decking. She also has an eight-foot-long boa constrictor living in a glass case in the kitchen.

Of the French gardens in *Visions of Roses* two stand out in my memory. The first is a garden high up in the mountains of the Alpes Maritimes above Grasse, owned by a Belgian, Bruno Goris. Access to this garden was difficult for me because I had to scramble up a very uneven rocky path that seemed to go on and upwards forever. The pathway is called Chemin du Paradis, very apt as I was struggling to get my breath! Goris lives in a converted shepherd's hut that had been built way back in 1820 and inherited the property from his parents who had used it as a holiday home. 'I was here before I was born' he said. Amongst the roses is the lovely, half-hardy 'Sénateur la Follette' (soft pink) and, one I had not seen before until then, 'Purezza', a repeat flowering, white hybrid of *Rosa banksiae*.

The other garden that impressed me in France belongs to the well-known French rose grower André Eve, its charm accentuated by the fact that it is tucked away behind a terrace house in Pithivier, an hour or so away from Paris. It was a pleasure to meet this noted rosarian. Neither of us could speak the other's language but it was marvellous how well we were able to communicate about our shared subject.

There are lots of good rose gardens in Italy. I was spoiled for choice for inclusion in the book. I will talk about just two of them here, the first being one I had already visited twice before. On the first occasion I was taken there by a rose friend, Elena Pizzi, and was then invited back to identify the many different roses growing in the gardens there by its curator, Lauro Marchetti. I will never tire of Ninfa. It is situated in Latina, about three hours' drive south from Rome.

The gardens at Ninfa were created between the 1950s and the mid-1970s by Lelia Caetani and her English husband Hubert Howard, building on restoration that was started by Lelia's family in the 1920s. The gardens were created from the ruins of a medieval city that fell into disrepair and became deserted in the late fourteenth century due to religious civil war followed by the plague. It remained in that state until early in the twentieth century. Within what remains of the old city walls are seven ruined churches, a lookout tower and a town hall, which has been restored as a Visitor Centre. Meandering and babbling its way through the garden is a little stream of crystal clear water that springs from the rocky escarpment to the north.

On my second visit Joan came with me and we enjoyed the privilege of staying overnight in the old Town Hall. I slept like a log but Joan was kept awake most of the night, hearing ghostly noises from the Old Hall part of the building and from the courtyard outside; the sound of feet hurrying past, the noise of horses and coaches arriving and departing and doors slamming.

The Ninfa experience is beyond mere words. Its ambience is one of peace and serenity. Almost, in this garden, time stands still. There are many impressive trees, flowering shrubs and a multitude of beautiful roses, amongst which I recall a delightful hedge of the double form of *Rosa roxburghii*, a glowing pink Species rose, the coppery-orange Tea rose, 'Général Schablikine', and some superb examples of the lovely, orange-yellow Noisette 'Desprez à Fleurs Jaunes'. The wide stream running along the length of the garden has three bridges and, so the legend goes, if you sit under the archway of one of the bridges, trail your hand in the cold, crystal clear water and close your eyes, you will experience the 'Spirito di Ninfa'. There is no other garden quite like it anywhere in the world.

During our stay there Lauro Marchetti received an invitation for us to accompany him to dinner at the fourteenth-century castle Terrecchia Vecchia from the owners, Prince Carlo Caracciolo and his wife Countess Violante Visconti. We heard later that the Prince owned the Italian newspaper *La Repubblica*. He had bought the 100-hectare estate blind, at an auction in Rome, as an investment. While having some of the extensive woodland cleared they came across a derelict castle, about which no documentation could be found anywhere in Italy. The Prince had the castle restored to its original state and uses it mainly as a weekend retreat.

There were twenty guests at this dinner and I mention it only in passing because of an embarrassing incident that took place. Joan was seated next to the Prince and, to her mortification, somehow managed to spill a full glass of red wine right over the white damask tablecloth. Confused, she did not know what to do. She apologised profusely and the Prince said 'It is-a-no trouble. To make amends you mus-a-kees every gentlemen seated at the table', which she did. At the end of a delightful evening we said our goodnights and Joan thanked the Prince for his wonderful hospitality. He raised her hand to his lips and said 'Thank you-a-Joan, for-a being you.' I suppose if one's wife must spill wine on anyone's tablecloth, it might as well be a Prince's.

The second Italian garden that I fell in love with is Villa Cetinale, just south of Siena, home of Lord Lambton and Claire Ward. (Lord Lambton, Under Secretary to the Minister of Defence in the Heath Government had left England in 1973 under a cloud, having confessed to a number of sexual indiscretions.) Although it is a beautiful garden it was really the history of the place that appealed to me most. The Villa nestles in the middle of an eighty-hectare estate that is situated on the side of a hill that rises from the south to its highest point in the north. It is no wonder that you can sense history everywhere in the Villa Cetinale and its gardens because there was an Etruscan presence on the site as far back as 800 BC. The large house was built in the fourteenth century and remodelled in the seventeenth century by Carlo Fontana, then a pupil of the great Italian architect Bernini.

Much of the estate is made up of ancient woodlands, mostly evergreen oaks. There is a 'stillness' here and the light, filtering through the trees, adds to the already ghostly ambience. Many paths, lined by moss-clad allegorical stone figures such as dragons, lions, tortoises and snakes, criss-cross their way through the forest. Claire Ward told me that the locals believe these woods are haunted. Pope Alexander VII spent a large part of his youth at Cetinale. In 1773 Fontana also designed a Hermitage that was built at the high north end of the estate. This can only be reached by climbing 250 narrow stone steps called the Scarla Santa. It is said that Flavio, a nephew of the Pope, murdered one of his rivals and, as a penance before he was allowed to become a cardinal, had to climb the Scarla Santa on his knees every day for a month.

16

USA *Sheriff, Macmillan Nurses and a Bimbo*

Another dog came into our lives in October 1996. Patchy had been dead for two years and when I asked Joan what she would like for her birthday, she replied 'A dog.' Although she loved Border collies, Joan felt that she would like a change. We were told about a litter of golden retrievers and, when we reached the kennels a few hours later, it was to find that there was only one puppy left, a boy dog. Frankly it would not have mattered if he had been ugly, Joan fell for him straight away and we drove back to Swangey Cottage with him cuddled up on her lap. She named him Oscar and he, in accordance with the canine pecking order, has become the most important member of our household.

'All work and no play makes Jack a dull boy' and so far I must have given the impression that I have done nothing with my life out-side the world of roses. My family, however, are very important to me and although I used to work long hours when the children were young, I always made time to take them on holiday, or to spend an occasional day at our favourite part of the North Norfolk coast. As a younger man I would take part in sport, especially football and cricket, but in latter years I have found snooker a good way to relax. I have never made a high break in this game but for two or three hours each week my friends and I compete in friendly rivalry.

Over the years, running the nursery has been like riding a seesaw, up one day, down the next. I had never had any business training but accountants, bank managers and business advisors were never shy in offering me advice. Had I listened to them I would have had to become a factory farmer growing only a small range of the most popular varieties in large quantities and by now would have made lots of money. In any case I have learned the hard way that bank managers only lend you an umbrella when the sun is shining. Having consistently ignored their advice I now have a collection of 1,300 different varieties of roses, with 300 or so of them rare and unique to us. In fact my company now has one of the biggest commercial collections in the world. I am proud to say that. The fact that it has been a constant struggle is neither here nor there. How can mere money compare to job satisfaction and the realisation of a dream? Money itself has never been important to me. As long as I can continue to invest in the future of the company, with enough to spare to provide my family with a comfortable lifestyle and a little left over, that is all I ask.

For us 1997 was a very busy year altogether. In early May I went by invitation to speak at a garden show in Carmel, California. The most memorable part of that event for me was driving my hired car to Carmel on the busy highway from Monterey Airport. It was a nightmare. I had no idea which road to take and I dare not look at my map. Horns were blasting away from behind and alongside me. Drivers were flashing their headlights at me, irritated by my lack of speed and the fact that I obviously didn't know where I was going. Eventually, in a cold sweat, I pulled up on the hard shoulder followed by a sheriff in a brightly coloured car. Hire cars in California have distinctive licence plates, so he already knew I was not a native. When I told him I was British he grinned and mumbled something about the wrong side of the road. He then asked me where I was going. 'Carmel' I said nervously. 'Follow me' he said and I had an escort all the way. By the time I was ready to make the return journey to the airport a week later I had regained my confidence.

In June we put on a display of our roses at a special Rose Weekend at Hex Castle in Belgium. This was the first time we had exhibited abroad. Hex Castle is the home of Comte Ghislain d'Ursel, and the gardens of his beautiful old château abound with roses. Since then we have visited Hex on several occasions and exhibiting there has become an annual event.

In the early 1990s the Royal National Rose Society formed a Historic Roses Group specifically for those of their members who were devotees of the older roses. Although I was not a founder member, I soon found myself on the committee. In late June 1997 the

Group organised an International Conference on Historic Roses. This was held at Cambridge and about 400 delegates from all around the world attended. I was asked to take the Chair. A gathering of 400 people of like minds is a recipe for a good time and we all enjoyed ourselves immensely. On the last evening a banquet was held in the famous medieval dining hall of King's College.

My next trip was to lecture at three different venues, two in Western Canada and one in Seattle. I flew to Vancouver to deliver the first lecture and was met there by Darlene Sanders, my driver for the duration of my stay. Darlene is a keen rosarian and has been a good friend ever since. From Vancouver I sailed on the ferry through beautiful island scenery to Victoria, where I did my second talk. I adore this part of the world. On my return to the mainland I was driven south through the lovely wooded landscape of Washington State to Seattle for my third presentation.

In July 1997, during Prince Charles's visit to our stand at Sandringham Flower Show, he mentioned in passing that he was Patron to the Macmillan Nurses Association and thought it would be nice if they could have a rose named for them. This was tantamount to a royal ommand. At Chelsea Flower Show 1998 we duly launched the rose 'Macmillan Nurse'. To receive the rose on their behalf, one of their nurses came to the stand to be photographed with it. It is one of the first varieties bred by Mandy and is a fully double white with a peachy centre.

For some time towards the end of 1997 I had been experiencing a few health problems, lots of abdominal pain and nausea. My GP sent me to see a specialist in Norwich who diagnosed a problem 'down below' that needed attention from his scalpel. However, as I was booked to lecture in Denmark in mid-January 1998 and he was going away on leave for a while, my operation was booked for later that month. Things did not go quite to plan and my operation actually took about eight hours. As the surgeon put it, 'I have had to remove about an arm's length of your intestine but don't worry you have more than enough left for your needs.' I remained in hospital for almost five weeks, eventually being allowed home in time to attend the AGM of the Norfolk and Norwich Horticultural Society, of which I was still President.

Now to my lecture in Denmark. This was the year after we had introduced a new rose called 'Horatio Nelson' a deep pink Shrub rose. There I was, in full flow, telling my audience in Copenhagen about the new rose when I suddenly remembered that Nelson had almost flattened this city with his cannons at the Battle of Copenhagen. I somehow managed to change the direction my lecture was taking but, by then, the damage was done. Afterwards I apologised for my lack of sensitivity to the Chairman of the Danish Rose Society. 'Think nothing of it,' he said, 'we should not have relied on the French!'

Before I left Copenhagen, like any tourist, I wanted to see the famous statue of the 'Little Mermaid' and was taken there by Torben Thim, a Danish rose nurseryman. When we found her, all we could see was a large wooden crate. We were told that a gang of vandals protesting against something or other had decapitated her the day before. So I had to be satisfied with looking at her picture in my guidebook.

The year we introduced 'Horatio Nelson' at the Chelsea Flower Show, we constructed, as the centrepiece of our stand, a large wooden bridge. It was quite tall, high above all the other stands nearby, and we had arranged roses all around it and built a sunken garden filled with roses beneath it. On this occasion we were again visited by John and Norma Major. To promote the rose our Manager Ian and his wife Tina dressed as Lord Nelson and Lady Hamilton and were standing on the bridge when the Majors arrived. Ian and Tina thoroughly enjoyed themselves and they certainly looked the part. We were all delighted to win another gold medal for this stand. Later that same year a bush of this variety was ceremoniously planted in the grounds of the church at Burnham Thorpe, where Nelson's father had been vicar.

On another occasion when I was in America I visited Heirloom Roses, Oregon, owned by John and Louise Clements. The Clementses own one of America's best-known rose nurseries, specialising in the Old roses. They also breed new roses and it was while inspecting some of their unnamed seedlings that my attention was drawn to a very free-flowering bright red shrub rose. I remarked how lovely it was and was then informed that, as I liked it, they would name it for me. This was a compliment I could not refuse and we exhibited 'Peter Beales' the rose for the first time at Chelsea Flower Show the following year.

My company was now selling a substantial number of roses to Japan each year. This all came about from the owners of Japanese garden centres visiting Chelsea Flower Show. They saw that our exhibit was rather different from the other rose stands at the show and they wanted to be able to sell our sort of roses in Japan. In 1998 Japan held an Exposition devoted to the UK, called UK '98. It was held at the Tokyo Forum, a very modern building, its interior modelled on the inside of a whale.

A part of the exhibition was devoted to gardening, English gardening in particular. Mr Yamada, the owner of Barakura English Garden, a Japanese garden centre and a very good customer of ours, invited me to exhibit roses on their behalf. This meant that a member of our company would have to reside in Tokyo for two months. Richard volunteered for this and he and I travelled to Tokyo together to attend the opening ceremony. It was opened jointly by the British Ambassador and the Japanese Trade Minister. The saki flowed freely and a good time was had by all. I stayed for just one week, leaving Richard in charge of the stand for the remaining seven weeks of the show.

It was while I was in Tokyo that my birthday came around. I think it must have been Richard who let this fact be known but halfway through the day Mr Yamada offered to take me out to dinner with some of his family. He gave me a choice of Western or Japanese cuisine. I chose Western. That evening we drove across Tokyo, eventually turning into a side street full of restaurants. The one we went into was called 'The 1066'. I soon learned that this was the only eating place in the whole of Tokyo that served traditional British dishes. The menu was full of such things as steak and kidney pie, roast beef and Yorkshire pudding, Lancashire hotpot and so on. I chose the hotpot and, as a compliment to me, so did the Yamada family, Eugene Yamada, his sister Miss Kaye and their elderly mother.

We all tucked in heartily and when it came time for dessert the choices were, amongst other things, spotted dick, bread and butter pudding and apple dumpling and custard. I chose the spotted dick, as did my fellow diners. The restaurant was full of British people, so imagine my surprise and embarrassment when the Yamada family all stood and sang to me, in their broken English, 'Happy birthday, dear Peter'. During this rendition a cake, with lots of lighted candles, arrived at the table and I was expected to blow them all out with one puff. As soon as the Yamada family started to sing all the other diners in the restaurant joined in with gusto. All I wanted to do was hide under the table. The whole Yamada family have since become cherished friends.

I returned to Japan the following year to go on a lecture tour around the Yamada's various garden shops. Starting in Tokyo I was escorted by the Barakura gardens manager, Mark Chapman, travelling by bullet train to Osaka, Kobe, Nagoya and Gifu. For this tour my guide was another one of the Yamada's employees, a young lady called Ikuko – I think! She spoke nearly perfect English and also acted as my translator when I lectured. I called her 'Nightingale' because when we were on an escalator at Nagoya Railway Station I fell and grazed my elbow quite badly. She promptly administered first aid and bandaged me up, hence 'Nightingale'. It was an easier name to remember than her real one. I have invented new names for my Japanese translators ever since because I can never remember their proper ones. I have delivered an annual lecture in Japan every year since 1998 and 'Rosie', 'Friday' and 'Kathy' are just three of the names I have called these girls. I know that they quite like this. It makes a refreshing change for them since everything in Japan is usually so very formal and proper.

Carrying on with the Japanese theme: in the autumn of 1998 I was commissioned to submit plans for the centrepiece stand at the Japanese Annual Rose Show, held in a baseball stadium called the Seibo Dome, just outside Tokyo. This meant two visits to Japan in 1999, the first in January to present my plans and attend press conferences etc and the second in May, to help supervise the putting up of the stand. I enjoyed this experience very much. The Japanese had adhered rigidly to my drawings and the finished garden exceeded my expectations. The Japanese way of showing emotion is far more expressive than that of Westerners. They loved the roses and their perfume and I was overwhelmed by the fact that many of the

Japanese ladies reacted to the stand with tears of joy. The fact that I had designed the main attraction at the show led on to healthy orders from several Japanese garden centres that year and the enhancement of our Company's image in Japan.

I mentioned earlier that I was a member of Rotary International. As such I am entitled to attend any Rotary Club meeting anywhere in the world. On one occasion whilst in Japan I accidentally got out of the lift in my hotel on the wrong floor to find myself in the reception area for a Rotary meeting. Good, I thought, I will introduce myself as a Rotarian from England and get a good meal into the bargain. I paid the equivalent of twenty pounds in Japanese yen to the Secretary and was shown to my seat, to a round of applause. This is normal for visitors in any Rotary Club. I sat down and my meal was served to me. It was a bowl of boiled rice and a glass of water. I had inadvertently dropped in at this Club's annual 'Charity Frugal Lunch'.

One day, in the early part of 1999, Gloria Hunniford contacted Mandy to ask about the possibility of naming a rose for the late Jill Dando. Gloria and her friend Sir Cliff Richard wanted this rose almost straightaway. We found a lovely single, scarlet Floribunda for them. The earliest it could be introduced was in July that year at Hampton Court Flower Show. Jill Dando had been a popular TV personality but had been shot, at close range, by a stalker. Both Gloria and Sir Cliff, who were Jill's close friends, came to the show for the very moving experience of launching the rose. Later that year we despatched bushes of her rose to be planted in Jill's Memorial Garden in her home town of Weston-Super-Mare.

That same year, because I am interested in sensory gardening, I was invited to become President of the Norfolk Gardening with Disabilities Charity. This was set up a few years ago by Tony Gipp and Elizabeth Kendal and now has a thriving membership. I take this office very seriously. Roses lend themselves well to sensory gardening because of their perfume.

As a country, New Zealand is high on my list of favourites and it so happens that it has a very active National Heritage Rose Society which, in turn, is divided into regional groups. On a visit to my nursery Joanne Knight, the then National President, invited me to lecture in five different venues throughout the length of the islands. I accepted of course, and the following November, their summertime, I set off for Auckland.

On arrival I went to visit my old friend Keith Money who had moved back to his native New Zealand a couple of years earlier. He was then living on a most delightful farm, about one hour's drive north of Auckland at Warkworth, having beautiful unspoilt views of undulating countryside all around. His garden was just what I expected – organised chaos but full of interesting plants, including some roses I was unable to name. Keith is not really interested in run of the mill varieties.

My first lecture was in Auckland, from where I was taken by car to Tauranga beside the Bay of Plenty, the venue for my second one. From there I flew down to Wellington and whilst there managed to visit Government House and take in a number of excellent rose gardens. From Wellington it was just a short hop by plane to Christchurch where I was met by a good friend, Barbara Lea Taylor, whom I knew from one of my previous visits to New Zealand. During my stay in this part of New Zealand Barbara was my guide and we enjoyed a diversion to the delightful little seaside town of Akaroa on the Banks Peninsula. My next destination was Dunedin. Were it not for the accent, it would have been easy, from the scenery, to imagine I was in Scotland.

The year 2000, on looking back, seemed to disappear like a flash. In January Joan and I flew to Pasadena, LA. Here at the invitation of Clair Martin, the Rose Curator at the Huntington Gardens, I spoke to a large audience of keen American rose lovers as the inaugural speaker in a new series of lectures, to be held annually, entitled 'Great Rosarians of the World'. These lectures are held at the famous Huntington Botanical Gardens, next door to the Huntington Library and Art Gallery. We took the opportunity to go and look at the Caxton Bible and Gainsborough's famous paintings *Blue Boy* and *Pinkie*. We packed a lot into that seven-day visit – museums and art galleries, including the Paul Getty, and, of course, a visit to Hollywood.

A year or two prior to this we had been asked by the vicar of Sandringham, Canon Hall, on behalf of the Sandringham Estate workers, if we could name a rose to commemorate the Queen Mother's centenary, due to take place in 2000. A climbing, creamy-white rose was selected by both the Canon and the Queen Mother, who, between them, had requested it be called 'Clarence House', the Queen Mother's London home for so many years. She was presented with this rose at Sandringham Flower Show a week or so before her hundredth birthday. It has since become one of our best-selling climbing roses.

I still had one rose left from my rose-breeding days. It is a tall growing, bright salmon-to-orange Floribunda with a superb perfume. In June 2001 my mother celebrated her eighty-fifth birthday and I decided to name this rose for her, calling it 'Evelyn May'. You can imagine how thrilled she was. Since being widowed Mum had become much more outgoing, almost feisty; in fact she totally regained her original personality. She and Rosie, who had never married, lived together and for each other at Buck Brigg and she helped Rosie to build up the North Norfolk branch of Peter Beales Roses. Sadly, through the latter years she was progressively unwell. In spite of being ill so very often towards the end she lived until just past her ninetieth birthday. Rosie, Joan, and myself were at her bedside at the end. On her bedside locker was a vase of 'Evelyn May' roses.

We introduced a rose called 'St Ethelburga' at Chelsea Flower Show 2002. It was named to celebrate the reopening of the London church of that name in Bishopsgate that was destroyed by an IRA bomb several years earlier. The newly built church is multi-denominational and, as such, is dedicated to reconciliation and peace. The Rt. Revd Richard Chartres, the Bishop of London came to our stand for its introduction. An amusing slant on this story is that all new roses are given code names these days before they are officially introduced to the world. The real Ethelburga had been a seventh-century abbess of Barking known as St Ethelburga the Virgin and had dedicated her life to saving girls of her day from prostitution. The rose 'St Ethelburga', oddly enough, had originally been given the code name 'bimbo'!

The little city of Oelde in Westfalen, Germany held a Rosefest in the summer of 2002. My company had designed and planted a new rose garden there and I was invited to attend. A well-known German brewery, Potts, has its headquarters in Oelde and, to the accompaniment of a German jazz band, the first rose was ceremoniously planted and anointed with a bottle of best German beer. Celebrations went on well into the night. To mark this occasion, I introduced a new semi-double, soft pink, Shrub rose bred by Amanda called 'City of Oelde'.

Mandy and Richard are both ambitious and want to move forward so, in 2002, we opened a garden shop and a bistro. These additional facilities mean that customers who visit us to buy rose bushes will be able to enjoy the gardens, purchase rose-related sundries and choose between either coffee and light refreshments or a three-course meal any day of the week.

17

Butterflies, Whales and Doves

In the spring of 2002 I became a Trustee of the Royal National Rose Society. I had heard rumours that the Society was floundering but it was not until I joined the Board that I became fully aware of just how serious things actually were. The RNRS, as it is known, is a charity and was founded in 1887 and by the 1920s had grown to become the biggest single genus society in the world. By the 1950s it rivalled the Royal Horticultural Society, RHS, for membership numbers. When I joined the Board these numbers had dropped to an all-time low, the Society's garden at St Albans had fallen into disrepair and the Society itself was existing on borrowed time.

Aware of all this, I will never know why in 2003 I found myself accepting the role of President. It soon became clear that I had taken on a very difficult task. The first thing I did was to put it to the Board that we needed the services of a business consultant to work with us and take over the role of chief executive. To this end we appointed Brian Gill and he and I hit it off from the word go. Hitherto the Board had consisted of rose devotees and horticulturists, none of whom had had very much, if any, financial or business experience. Such was the state of affairs that, at this same meeting, we had to decide if, under company law, the Society could carry on, as it was clear that it was close to insolvency.

To compound the problems, the Society had been in the process of courting an American fundraiser who had promised several million pounds to fund the building of a new rose garden. The idea was that this money was to be raised in America from sponsorship on the back of naming the new garden 'The Princess Diana Memorial Garden'. To date no money at all had been forthcoming and I became suspicious. It seemed too good to be true and I made it a condition of my Presidency that all contact with the American fundraiser be dropped. In the event my suspicions proved to be correct and the whole project went sour, bringing the Society almost to its knees.

At some point, when the American debacle was still going on, the Society's activities had been reported to the Charity Commission by one of its members and, when I became President, they were already in the middle of investigating its affairs. They were dubious about the whole American fundraising scheme and were concerned about the legal aspect of it. In the early negotiations with the fundraiser lots of publicity had been generated, publicity which promised a glowing future for the Society and its rose gardens. Little wonder that optimism and enthusiasm had clouded the Board's thinking.

When the press heard of the collapse of this fundraising scheme their mood changed from positive to negative overnight. By then the Board of Trustees was divided, some of them still believing in the American dream and others, including myself, facing up to reality. Just before I came on the scene, this dissent caused the resignation of two members of the Board. Even then the Trustees remained divided and there was some acrimony at Board meetings. Part of the Board were for reopening negotiations with the fundraiser because they still wanted to believe that it was the answer to all the Society's problems. They had been sold the idea by the charismatic and very persuasive American lady.

The Board meetings, to say the least, were contentious with individual Trustees having a go at each other, but even though I had to thump the table a few times, those in favour of the American alliance continued to be disruptive. It became clear to me that, even with them being in a minority it would be difficult to move the Society forward with the Board at loggerheads. Clearly the answer was to change the personnel somehow. Three of the longer-serving Trustees, as they came to the end of their term of office, opted for retirement. This gave me the opportunity to recruit people of the right calibre on to the Board, people who were not steeped in and hung up on the old ways and would therefore be able to see the way forward clearly. Without all the previous arguments it was now possible to make constructive decisions and render the Society viable once more.

In due course the Charity Commission found that the Society had been wrong to pursue funds via the American fundraiser. However, there was little they could do about it, as their jurisdiction did not extend to the USA. Anyway they gave the Board of the RNRS their blessing to move forward.

The Society was cash poor and asset rich, owning as it did a large house and twenty-five acres in the middle of Hertfordshire. I must say that before I came on the scene the then Board had worked hard in getting planning permission for the building of the 'Memorial Garden'. They had also acquired additional land, bought from an adjoining farm. Although this was sound business sense had the funds been raised in America, it was the cost of this purchase plus legal fees etc that was mainly responsible for the current sad state of the finances.

The new Board decided that the way forward was to find a buyer for half the estate and use the funds released by this to build a new garden and bring the Society back to where it should be, the leading Society in the world of roses. Once it became known that the land was up for sale we had one or two quite serious offers from property developers, one of whom wanted to turn the site into a theme park. This was a good offer and we were on the verge, albeit reluctantly, of accepting it when a charity called 'Butterfly World' came on the scene, wanting to buy the land to build a Butterfly Biome. The ethos of this idea appealed to the Board as a symbiotic relationship could be formed by the two charities, with visitors having the option of enjoying both the gardens and the Butterfly Biome. Following protracted discussions the Trustees agreed to sell to Butterfly World.

Once the sale was completed and we had received the money, we commissioned the well-known garden designer Michael Balston to draw up plans for the new garden. These plans were approved, and landscape gardeners Adam Frost Ltd built the gardens. The roses for the new gardens were all donated by members of the British Rose Growers Association. By now my two-year term of office had ended. I, along with my fellow Trustees, had accomplished more than I had ever dared hope for. The new President, Ann Bird, has presided over the rebuilding of the gardens and they reopened to members of the RNRS and the general public in June 2007.

One of my first social duties as President was to represent the Rose Society at the World Federation of Rose Societies Convention in Glasgow in July 2003. This was a four-day event opened by Princess Anne. Following her speech declaring the Convention open, it fell to me to thank her on behalf of the Federation. Over my years working with roses I have had to make several speeches, but this – dauntingly – was the first time I had had to follow royalty.

By now Richard was adept at designing our stands at both Chelsea and Hampton Court and we all knew that the stand we put up to his design at Chelsea 2003 was outstanding. When we arrived at the stand at eight o'clock on the Tuesday morning to see what award we had been given (the medal cards are placed on the stands overnight) we found that we had been awarded a gold medal. We were so busy drinking champagne to celebrate the 'gold' that we did not notice the envelope placed next to the medal card. It was not until one of the judges called at the stand to congratulate us on our awards that I discovered the envelope and found that it contained a note from the President of the RHS, Sir Richard Carew-Pole. The note stated that he would be calling at the stand at eleven o'clock that morning to present us with the 'President's Award for the best stand in the Show'. This was the first year this award had been presented. All the family and the staff were ecstatic and I was rendered speechless. Receiving this award meant that we had a good reason to open yet another bottle of champagne.

Subsequently, in July of that year, we were also awarded the 'President's Trophy for the best stand in the Rose Marquee' at Hampton Court Flower Show. Once again it was an excuse for the champagne to flow. We all thought that this was the last chance of winning anything else that year. However, to our delight, in December, after all the shows had finished, we received a letter informing us that we had been awarded the 'Lawrence Medal' as our Chelsea stand had been adjudged the best stand at any of the RHS shows for that year.

At Christmas 2003 the family were all gathered together and relaxing after a festive lunch when Mandy produced the proofs for our next catalogue. She asked Joan if she would mind casting a quick eye over them and I could tell that she found this request a little odd for Christmas Day, of all days. Joan opened the front cover. After a brief silence, with tears in her eyes, she said 'Who is responsible for this?' The rest of the family had plotted together to name a rose 'Joan Beales', to be introduced to the world at Chelsea Flower Show 2004. The rose is fragrant, semi-double, deep velvety red with pronounced golden stamens and a spreading, shrubby growth habit. The launch was a happy occasion. Unbeknown to Joan, Mandy had arranged with Joan's sister Christine to come to Chelsea that day and actually present her rose to her at the stand on behalf of the family.

Also that year we introduced another royal rose, 'Countess of Wessex'. The rose had been named at the request of the Rt. Revd Peter Nott, retired Bishop of Norwich, for whom we had introduced the rose 'Norwich Cathedral' a few years earlier. He had officiated at the wedding of the Earl and Countess. This rose is superbly scented and soft creamy-white in colour.

Later that summer Mandy and her family moved back to Norfolk from Oxford, where they had lived for several years. During her time in Oxfordshire she had continued to work for our company, fulfilling her role as marketing director and rose breeder. It is so good to have her back in Norfolk and she has been able to re-establish herself as part of the team. She clearly has the knack for rose breeding, as amongst her seedlings are some very promising varieties. On the marketing side she plays a major part in the design and layout of our catalogue. She has also taken it upon herself to oversee our web site, which is recognised as one of the best and most informative sites within the rose industry. Another plus of having Mandy living nearby is that Joan and I can spend more time with our grandchildren, Laura and Alex.

Soon after my annual visit to Barakura English Garden, Japan in June 2004, Joan and I travelled by car to the beautiful city of Trier in Southern Germany near the border of Luxembourg. Trier is the birthplace of one of Germany's most famous rose breeders of the nineteenth century, Peter Lambert. As you would expect there is a lovely rose garden in this city, containing a large number of roses bred by him. I was there to give a lecture to local rose lovers.

Trier, the oldest city in Germany, has many interesting buildings, lots of which date back to Roman times, including the 'Porta Nigra', the Roman gateway into the city. The most memorable part of our stay was when our hosts took us for a trip on a pleasure boat on the Moselle river that threads its way through Luxembourg to join the Rhine at Koblenz. All along the riverbanks are acres and acres of vineyards sloping gently towards the river. We stopped at Bernkastel-Kues for lunch, a beautiful little town where we partook of a few glasses of Mosel wine, from the same vines we had passed while on our boat trip. Then we all climbed aboard a mountain railway train with open carriages to ascend to the restaurant in the courtyard of the ruins of Landshut Castle, perched on the top of a small mountain. From this castle the views all around were fantastic.

My fifth book, *A Passion for Roses*, was published in time for Easter 2004. It had been written piecemeal throughout the previous two years. It is much more personalised than my earlier books, dealing as it does with only my favourite roses.

Chelsea Flower Show 2005 saw the introduction of two more of our new roses. One was 'Gardener's Joy' to celebrate the 400th anniversary of the London Livery Company, the Worshipful Company of Gardeners. This is a champagne-coloured, perfumed shrub rose. The launch of 'Gardener's Joy' however was rather overshadowed by our other new introduction.

We had not meant this to happen but the press decided that our second new rose, named 'Sir John Mills', was more newsworthy. The famous actor had passed away only a few days before the show. Sir John's family had asked us to breed a rose for him a year or so earlier. Knowing that he would not be able to come to the show because of his deteriorating health, we delivered some blooms of his rose to him at his home and he was able to see and smell it before he passed away. His two daughters Juliet and Hayley received the rose on his behalf and it was a moving event.

We had been living at Swangey Cottage for fourteen years and had been very happy there. However we had finally obtained planning permission to build a bungalow on a part of the nursery. With old age creeping up we decided that now was the right time to build.

We approached a lifelong friend, Mike Smithers, an architect, to draw up the plans. Obviously we had a big input in the design and work started in earnest in the summer of 2004. We moved into 'Pippins', as our new home is called, at Easter 2005.

Over the months preceding our move the family, as directors of Peter Beales Roses Ltd, had been in discussion with Paul Zimmerman of Ashdown Roses, South Carolina, planning a way forward for an alliance of our two companies. I had always felt that we needed to find a means of promoting and marketing our roses in America and a partnership of this type seemed to be the obvious route to take, especially as both parties were keen to cement the alliance more securely. After a couple of reciprocal visits, Paul to us and Richard to Ashdown, a business plan evolved and we sent our first cuttings to Paul at Ashdown in the summer of 2005. Our roses are therefore now available on their own roots from Ashdown Roses and each of our web sites have pictures and descriptions of most of the roses raised both by myself in the 1970s and 1980s and by Mandy more recently. Richard and Mandy are carrying out much of the spadework and promotional activities for this alliance in association with Paul and his team. For my part, I am thrilled to know that after all these years we have a viable presence in America. It so happened that, concurrent with our discussions with Paul to forge the alliance, Ashdown Roses was building a relationship with a company called Organic Plant Health Care who have developed a completely natural Rose Care Programme to be launched in 2008. I am honoured that my signature will be endorsing these products.

In June that year I set off to Canada to take part in the Fiftieth Anniversary celebrations of the Canadian Rose Society. The invitation came from their President, Rachel Flood, and for the first weekend I stayed with her and her husband Ken at their home in Kitchener near Toronto. They were to be my travelling companions and guides for the two-week lecture trip across Canada.

The first lecture was at the Hamilton Botanical Gardens, Toronto. From there our next port of call was Halifax, Nova Scotia. There we stayed in the Nelson Hotel, a small reminder of Norfolk for me. From Halifax we flew to Montreal where my lecture took place at the famous Botanical Gardens. Montreal is where Ken was born and he and Rachel took me on a tour of this fascinating city. The day of my lecture coincided with London learning that it had been awarded the 2012 Olympics. This was a surprise as Paris had been the favourite up until then. With Montreal being a French-Canadian city there were several long faces at the reception later that evening.

Next stop Calgary, arriving just in time, as our plane had been delayed at Montreal. I have pleasant memories of having lunch with the Calgary Rose Society members, in a revolving restaurant at the top of the Communications Tower there. From this high point, as the restaurant revolved, we could see the vast distance of the prairies spread out to the east and the foothills of the Rockies to the west. From here, it was over the Rocky Mountains by plane to Vancouver where, once again, I met lots of old friends. From Vancouver it was just a short flight over the islands to Victoria for my last lecture. Whilst in this city we were taken to Government House to take tea with the Lieutenant Governor of British Columbia, Iona Campagnolo.

With all my lectures behind me, some friends of the Floods arranged for us all to go whale watching on a seagoing yacht. We saw one or two pods of whales surfacing and cavorting in the choppy waters of the Straits of Georgia. The coastline, viewed from the boat, was rugged and dramatic. The next day it was back to Toronto, en route for home. One of the big pluses of my Canadian lecture tour is the friendship that has grown between my family and that of the Floods. Both Ken and Rachel have become shareholders in our company.

2005 was the 125th anniversary of Colby School, which, you recall, was where I first started school. One of the school governors suggested that, as I was an old boy, it would be nice if I could name a rose for the school. The new rose was unveiled on the day of the anniversary. Visiting the school after such a long time was quite a moving experience. On going into the first year classroom again, I made straight for the corner of the room and stood facing the wall, just as I had done so many, many times as a pupil.

Joan often laughs and says that, throughout our married life, she has always had to take second place to roses and in many ways this is true – I have enjoyed a lifelong affair with them from the early days at LeGrice's up to the present time. I am of course biased but no other flower can rival the rose for its abundance of virtuous qualities. I love all roses but, inevitably, I have my favourites. I particularly like the form of many of the old varieties such as the Gallicas, Albas and Centifolias of all shades, especially when this classical shape is linked to perfume. Such roses, in my eyes, come close to perfection. Having said this, there is no such thing as a 'perfect rose'; roses are individuals and they all have their foibles but these only tend to make each one more intriguing.

My love affair with roses started with 'Maiden's Blush' when I was a child, I was totally overwhelmed by its beauty and perfume. Later, in my teens, I learned that this rose had originally come from France where it was known as 'Cuisse de Nymphe Ému' (Thigh of the Passionate Nymph). You can imagine how I felt when I learned that I had fallen for a rose with such an evocative name. As time passed and I learned more and more about roses and their evolution I developed a special fondness for the wild roses of Nature, from all parts of the world. I find their simplicity and purity very appealing.

I find it fascinating that roses of all types have evolved from Nature's pure roses, mostly by man-manipulation. The story of 'The Rose' unfolds through the virginal yet scintillatingly seductive single roses to the multi-petalled older varieties that embrace both the blowsy old tarts and the voluptuous 'Madames'. Using the same analogy I see the modern roses as brightly made up chorus girls and flamboyant fandango dancers with here and there a few quieter varieties, which remind me of elegant ballet dancers. Also amongst the ranks of modern roses are the so-called 'blue' varieties. I can see why some rose lovers desire these but since blue is not a natural pigment in the makeup of a rose I am far too much of a purist ever to want to see a bed of bright blue roses.

Perfume, to me, is an important attribute for any rose and I can never come across a rose without putting my nose amongst its petals to sniff it. I am not alone in this. Even toddlers just beginning to walk will instinctively put their faces into roses and smell them.

The rose has featured in social history almost since the beginning of time and poets, songwriters and artists have immortalised it in their works. It gives me a great deal of satisfaction to know that my passion for roses is shared by many people worldwide and is England's favourite flower.

June 2005 was the thirtieth anniversary of the founding of our company. While I was away in Canada my family and staff had organised a party to celebrate the occasion. They invited friends, relatives and many customers of long standing. It was a beautiful, sunny day. The roses were gorgeous and our glasses overflowed. At the party we met Richard's future wife Debbie for the first time. The following year they were married and she is a very welcome addition to the family and, even more wonderful, we now have a new, lovely little granddaughter called Maddie.

As past President of the Royal National Rose Society I received an invitation to attend the 7th World Federation of Rose Societies Conference in Osaka, Japan in mid-May 2006. I was one of about 400 delegates and I found myself rubbing shoulders with rosarian friends from all over the world. My return flight did not get into Heathrow until the evening of Press Day at Chelsea Flower Show. This was the first year ever that I had not been involved in putting up the stand and also the first time I had missed a rose launch. I went to the Show early on the Tuesday morning and discovered that we had been awarded a gold medal – it only goes to show that no one is indispensable! I accompanied Mandy and Richard to the exhibitors' bar to celebrate the award. While standing at the bar I began to have pains in my chest. At first I thought I had indigestion but the pains did not go away, they got worse. Mandy and Richard thought I ought to get medical advice. One of them had to stay at the Show and it was decided that Mandy would accompany me to the nearest hospital. A taxi was called and the driver took us to the A & E Department at St Thomas' Hospital. I was immediately admitted to one of the cardiac wards and within a few hours underwent an angioplasty. After this I felt so much better, my breathing had improved and I had no pain. After six days I was allowed to go home.

I was due to return to Japan for my usual annual trip some three weeks after the day of my operation. My family did not want me to go although the hospital had told me it was safe to fly. I was in a difficult position. On one hand I understood my family's concern but was adamant that I could not let the Yamada family down at such short notice. In the end Joan insisted that she would come with me. Our week's stay in Japan was without incident, in fact I felt extremely well. As with other visits here, when it came time to leave, my hosts showered me with gifts, amongst these were two bottles of a new Japanese health drink, blueberry vinegar, that I had been invited to taste and said I thought was delicious. As well as our luggage we now had numerous carrier bags full of gifts and we had to travel by train to Tokyo. At Chino station I decided to put these bottles into the top of my rucksack for safety. When we boarded the train we placed our luggage in the luggage compartment behind our seats and settled down for the journey. After about ten minutes I spotted two or three little rivulets of dark red liquid flowing past my feet. At first I thought it was blood but then the penny dropped and I nudged Joan for her to take a look. It was clearly our blueberry vinegar.

Japanese trains are spotless so, obviously, we had to do something about cleaning it up. By now the rivulets had trickled quite a way and the other passengers had noticed them. While I attended to the rucksack Joan grabbed a load of paper towels from the nearby WC and getting down on her hands and knees attempted to wipe up the mess. Very elegant, an English lady on her knees in a Japanese train. Soon the ticket collector appeared in his spotless white uniform. Communication with him was impossible so, using sign language, we tried to explain what had happened. He was clearly not amused by our predicament but nevertheless proceeded to assist us with the clearing up, again with paper towels from the toilet. I had managed to remove the broken bottles from my rucksack by now and I hastily wrapped these in a plastic carrier bag and disposed of them in a waste bin in the entrance to the compartment. When we finally reached our hotel we discovered that most of the contents of my rucksack were stained beyond recovery. Our fellow Japanese passengers were very understanding and amused but this did not take away our embarrassment.

This seems to me a good place to bring this story to an end. At our thirtieth anniversary celebration my family and staff had presented me with six, pure white, fantail doves. Now, as they tumble and swoop over the rose gardens, they somehow help me to forget all the negatives of the years gone by and remind me just how very fortunate I am to have been able to spend my life with roses.